# The Death Penny

Anthony Bartlett

Published by New Generation Publishing in 2025



First Edition



Paperback ISBN 978-1-83563-676-3
Hardback ISBN 978-1-83563-677-0

**www.newgeneration-publishing.com**

New Generation Publishing

# CONTENTS

CHAPTER 1 4
South London - 1916

CHAPTER 2 20
South London - 1970

CHAPTER 3 36
Catterick – 1916

CHAPTER 4 58
Lenders and Debtors – 1916

CHAPTER 5 80
Robert McKenzie

CHAPTER 6 98
The Investigation Continues - 1970

CHAPTER 7 110
The Investigation Commences - 1916

CHAPTER 8 122
The Investigation Continues

CHAPTER 9 138
Secrets

CHAPTER 10 154
Process of Elimination - 1916

CHAPTER 11 170
Half Term - 1970

CHAPTER 12 190
The Reluctant German

CHAPTER 13 206
Fix Bayonets

CHAPTER 14 224
Going Home

CHAPTER 15 242
More Agony, More Tragedy

CHAPTER 16 252
A Policeman's Lot Is Not A Happy One

CHAPTER 17 266
Case Closed

CHAPTER 18 280
South London - 1945

CHAPTER 19 288
The Truth Revealed

EPILOGUE 304

CHAPTER

# 1

# SOUTH LONDON - 1916

The knock on the door of number 5 Queens buildings could only mean one thing. It came every Saturday on the stroke of twelve without fail.

Charlie Williams was sitting in the back kitchen slouched over a bowl of his wife Betty's hot stew and a large crust of bread after coming in from the usual back-breaking shift at the Pegg coal yard. These days, he wasn't sure if more was being crammed into the half-hundred-weight bags or if he was simply getting older. Either way, it was a hard job and it was getting harder now that his boys had left home to join up. He'd worked in the coal yard for the last twenty-five years and more and more he found himself wondering how long he could carry on. Straining his back with that delivery to Manor Place last week didn't help either – he'd been in pain ever since. Now this.

Betty was in the communal wash house out the back, winding Charlie's sodden, discoloured shirts through the mangle. As she stood in the murky puddles on the stone floor, her mind inevitably wandered towards her two boys, Len and Reg, conscripted and sent to Catterick for training prior to deployment. She had hardly enjoyed a night's sleep since they left.

Eighteen months ago, nobody had ever heard of some bloke called Archduke Ferdinand; no one knew of any problems in the Balkans, wherever *they* were; and everyone was ignorant of the various European alliances that would see one country supporting one side or another in times of conflict. But everyone was now aware that the country had been dragged into a war that the ordinary people knew nothing about. And it was the young men of the country who had been ordered to fight it. The guttural scream that came out of Elsie Dorkins at number 23 when she heard her son had been killed in France remained lodged in Betty's mind. Like the other inhabitants of the Queen's Buildings tenement, she had fallen silent when she heard Elsie's agonising shriek – everyone had known immediately what it meant.

Betty's thoughts were broken when she heard a loud banging on the front door. "Are you getting that?" she called over her shoulder.

"Yes," came Charlie's irritated reply through the open back door.

He pushed his bowl away, hauled himself up from his chair, stretched by thrusting his fists into the small of his back and trailed towards the front door, fully aware of who was on the other side.

"Hello Charlie!" said the smug Billy Connor as the door opened. "How you keeping? Just come for the weeklies."

Charlie looked at the young man with contempt: podgy, round-faced with his fancy waistcoat and bowler hat tipped back on his head, notebook and pencil at the ready.

"You'll have to come back later," he snarled through gritted teeth.

"If I have to come back later, there'll be interest added."

Charlie needed all his self-control not to plant one on the grinning leech. "You really love to see the misery of others, don't you?"

"Well, when you come to us in the first place, you know the rules, Charlie boy. Times a bit harder are they, since your two boys left? Maybe it won't be long before your Maureen can help out."

At the mention of his sons and daughter, Charlie snapped and lurched towards Connor, almost knocking his hat from his head. "Don't you ever mention my daughter's name!" he shouted. "And while I'm about it, why aren't you and that useless brother of yours doing your bit, eh? Too busy feeding off the honest hard work of others – you and that crooked father of yours. Who did he bribe to keep you two idiots from being conscripted?"

The younger man wrestled with the clenched fists that had hold of his lapels. "You can't speak to me like that" was his pathetic response as he managed to break himself free. "My dad will be hearing about this."

"Yeah, piss off to your dad and tell Jack he will get his money next week!"

The flustered boy scampered away from the blackened tenement, wondering how he was going to explain to his father that he hadn't collected all this week's debts. For now, however, he just needed to get away – off he ran down London Bridge Road, occasionally glancing behind him to see if Charlie Williams was following.

People had started to spill out onto the street to see what all the fuss was about. When they saw their tormentor scurrying along, there was many a smile behind a hand, but no one dared laugh or cheer for

fear of payback from the notorious Connor family.

Money lenders were nothing new: when ordinary people had nothing left to pawn, they would go to individuals they knew could help them out and tide them over till payday. But in recent years, and especially since the war broke out, things had got worse. Those same individuals who once helped a few people out had now developed small empires and ruled their particular area with a rod of iron. Merciless in their terms, unforgiving in their retribution. The Connors were typical of the breed – they were needed by many among the poor, working-class South London community but were detested by everyone for their bullying and viciousness.

When Billy Connor had disappeared from sight,

many gestured their approval towards Charlie, who acknowledged them with an upward nod before going back inside. He stood with his back to the closed door and wondered what the bloody hell he had just done – he may have enjoyed a momentary victory over that snivelling little Billy, but he still owed his father, Jack Connor, money: money that he didn't have and money that he wasn't likely to get any time soon.

Much as he hated to admit it to himself, there was an element of truth in what Billy had said about his boys leaving to join up. Their wages had helped with the running of the house but now Charlie was the main provider. In the absence of young men, young women were now being employed to take their places in the factories and Maureen had got a job at the Woolwich Arsenal armaments factory, but as women were being paid less than the men they replaced, her contribution to the household bills was limited. He also knew, in his heart of hearts, that his own drinking habits didn't help: Friday was payday and Friday night meant The George.

"Who was that?" asked Betty as she came in from the back yard with a bundle of washing.

It was pointless lying; the two had been together nearly twenty-five years and Betty knew Charlie inside out. They had met when Charlie worked as a young lad with Betty's dad, Bob Reeves, at the coal yard. Every year, Pegg & Company organised a charabanc trip to Margate for the workers and their families. It was on one such trip in August of 1891 that Bob had brought his daughter, Betty, along. While the majority of those on the outing went swimming and took donkey rides, Charlie and Betty just sat on the beach talking and sharing the odd ice cream, oblivious to the giddy shouts and screams of those playing in the sea and the tunes from the hurdy-gurdy man entertaining the crowds. Bob knew Charlie was a bit rough round the edges, but he also knew he was a good lad at heart. He approved of the two being together and two years later, the young couple were married.

Twenty-three years on, they were now a middle-aged couple with three adult children. For all of their faults – mainly Charlie's – they still thought the world of each other. And like most married couples of such standing, the two knew each other's every mannerism, every unspoken word.

"The Connors," said Charlie in answer to his wife's question – this was a regular occurrence. Before Betty could ask anything further, there was another knock on the door. Charlie opened it to find his next-door neighbour Tommy Black standing with a big grin on his face.

"Good lad, Charlie, it's about time someone put that boy in his place."

Charlie was aware that his neighbour had received similar threats from the Connors, and during one conversation it had been suggested that Maggie – Tommy's daughter – could assist in other ways if Tommy

didn't have the money he owed readily available. Charlie never did ask what the eventual outcome was. Nor did he follow up on the rumours around the impoverished tenements that women who had lost their husbands in the war were being harassed by these despicable creatures in lieu of monies owed. He couldn't be sure exactly what was behind Billy Connor's comment about his own daughter "helping out", but it made his flesh creep. A few other pleasantries were exchanged before Tommy returned to his own door.

"What happened?" asked Betty, alarmed.

"I had words with Billy Connor and sent him on his way."

"And did you pay him?" The silence was deafening. "You didn't pay him? What are we going to do now then? You were in that bloody George again last night, weren't you, drinking your wages away. What are we supposed to do now?" she repeated.

"I'll think of something."

"Well, you better think of something fast or we'll be out on the street."

Like other families around the country, the Williams had had to tighten their belts since war had been declared: the cost of meat had gone up, while flour, sugar, tea and cheese had all doubled in price. Before Betty could lay into her husband still further, they were interrupted by Maureen, returning home for her lunch.

"Everyone seems in good spirits," she said as she entered, "they're all up and down the street laughing and joking with one another. What's going on?"

"Nothing, love," said her mother, "come and have your dinner, I've got some stew on the stove."

"Any news from the boys?" asked Maureen. At twenty-one, she was the oldest of the three children and enjoyed her role as the big sister.

"Mary received a letter from Len yesterday," said Betty, "she brought it round to show us this morning."

"*Ooh*, writing to Mary, is he?" said Maureen in mock offence.

"The two seem really sweet on each other."

"Yes, I know" – Maureen leaned in closely to her mother and lowered her voice, as though what she was about to say was top secret – "I saw Mary the other day. She told me that she hoped Len was going to propose to her when he gets back."

"I hope so," said Betty, "she's a lovely girl. I just hope they get the chance before he goes away again." There was more than a hint of concern in her voice and she dropped her head as the worried expression enveloped her face once more.

Everyone had been told that this business would

all be over by Christmas: that had been eighteen months ago and there was still no sign of an end to it all. The reality was that it was getting worse. For over a year, endless thousands of men and boys had been shipped across to France, and newspaper reporters that followed them were not sugar-coating the details of the mud, filth and slaughter they were encountering when they arrived.

The country was in uproar as a result: every day, wives and families dreaded the arrival of an official-looking letter that would bring the most feared news possible. What had started off as telegrams to a few grief-stricken families in the early months of the war had now turned into hundreds of buff-coloured envelopes delivered with the morning post. It was such a delivery that had led to Elsie screaming out her agony three months earlier. Betty hurried round to find the poor woman collapsed on her kitchen floor, grasping the note that informed her that her only child had been lost.

"What did he say?" asked Maureen, referring to her brother's letter while trying to rescue her mother from her dark thoughts.

"Oh, he says that he and Reg are bored with the training. They've been there a few weeks now and are itching to get away. They're safer where they are if you ask me," said Betty.

Charlie had been only half-listening to his wife and daughter chatting between themselves. His mind was on the Connors and how he was going to get the money he owed them before they decided to make some alternative arrangements. Twelve months earlier, he had borrowed five pounds off Jack Connor when food prices had gone up. He knew that many in his tenement and others up and down the street regularly dealt with the moneylenders, so he had gone into the arrangement with his eyes open. Vowing never to get trapped in the never-ending lending and borrowing cycle endured by some of his neighbours, Charlie had paid off his debt over the following five months and promised himself he wouldn't get caught up with those odious people again. Two months ago, however – after much soul-searching since the boys had left and spending days justifying his change of mind to himself – he had gone back to them and borrowed another fiver. He had struggled ever since to make the weekly repayments and hated himself for wasting some of his wages at the pub. But he couldn't help himself what else was there in these desperate times?

As her mother went through to the kitchen to warm up the stew, Maureen asked, "You all right, Dad?" It was clear that her father was miles away.

Charlie snapped out of his thoughts. "Yes, I'm fine love. How was your morning?"

"Oh, the usual deafening! I don't know what it's like at the front, but there's certainly plenty of banging and crashing when we're making the damn things!"

They both fell silent and looked through to see if Betty had heard Maureen's indiscreet comment. It dawned on them both that Len and Reg would soon be experiencing the war first-hand and as concerned as they both were, they knew Betty was beside herself with worry at the thought.

"Sorry," whispered Maureen to her dad, "I could cut my tongue out!"

"Don't worry about it love, I don't think Mum heard." Charlie hugged his daughter and kissed her on the forehead. "I tell you what, let's go through and finish our dinner."

As the two walked through to the back, he thought to himself how much better he was becoming at putting on an act.

Pegg & Co Coal Merchants

The Smug Billy Connor

Munitions Workers at the Woowich Arsenal Munitions Factory

# CHAPTER

# 2

# SOUTH LONDON - 1970

It was two days before the start of the summer holidays. Two days – and then no more of this for six long weeks. Next year would be the final year, which meant it would start with mock O-Levels in September and would end with the real thing next year. But all that could wait.

Best friends Tony and Mickey sat in the class and were only paying lip service to old "Smithy" by this point. They were full of the World Cup that had just finished: Gordon Banks had made that save from Pelé but it hadn't stopped Brazil from winning the Jules Rimet Trophy for the third time, which, the boys agreed, was a bit greedy. Both their mums had let them watch some of the matches late at night, beamed live from Mexico. They were now looking forward to spending the next six weeks in Kennington Park, recreating some of the skills they'd witnessed from those footballers with their exotic-sounding names from around the world.

"Are you boys paying attention?" demanded Mr Smith of the two.

"Oh, yes, sir," said Tony, breaking away from his whispering with Mickey.

Tony eyed the history teacher up and down – he was difficult to age, was our Mr Smith, he could be anything between fifty and eighty. Typical teacher, never seen out of the old brown jacket and the dusty black trousers that didn't quite fit him properly; he seemed permanently covered in chalk. For his part, Mr Smith looked out at his class and wore an expression that suggested he was as tired of them as they were of him. Years of teaching the same curriculum to kids, half of whom had no interest in history at all.

"Now, to keep your minds active over the summer," he said finally, "I want you to do a local history project and hand it in on the first day back."

The whole class wore the same expression of shock and disbelief. It was the summer holidays! Why would they want to do more schoolwork during the summer holidays? Was he for real?

It was as if Mr Smith had read their thoughts. "Next year is your biggest school year. You need to be sharp throughout and this will prove a good start."

"What do you want us to write about?" asked one of the boys.

"Anything to do with local history. Utilise the library and museums. Oh, and one last thing – no football!"

"But—" started Mickey and then thought better of it.

With that, Mr Smith strode out of the class, followed by his usual trail of chalk dust.

So, that was that – the class trooped out believing

the summer holidays had just got one week shorter thanks to Mr Smith. Tony and Mickey hadn't got a clue what they were going to write about. Kennington was . . . well . . . Kennington, as good as anywhere else but nowhere of note.

"What's wrong with your face?" asked Tony's mum when he got home. He explained what Mr Smith had asked them to do. "Well, you'll think of something," was the classic mother's response. *Thanks, Mum,* thought her son.

A few days of moping around saw Tony into the summer holidays with still no real idea of what he could write about. His mood wasn't lightened any when Mickey told him that he was going to write about the burning down of Crystal Palace in 1936.

"That's local history," said Mickey triumphantly.

The only thing Tony could think of was asking his dad about the war, but when his father told him that he had just been a driver, carrying out fairly mundane duties, it proved another dead end. It was then that his mum stepped in and saved the day.

"Why don't you go and see your nan – she's lived round here all her life. If there are any stories to tell, Nan will know about them."

Nanny Eames was born in 1897 and had lived in Queen's Buildings all her life. At seventy-three years old and just over five feet tall, although looking frail, she was very sprightly for her age. She lived in the next tenement block and was known throughout the area as a matriarchal figure who had always helped the community. She wasn't exactly a grandmother to Tony but when his natural grandmother had died giving birth to Tony's mum, it was Nanny Eames who had raised her. She had always been a constant in Tony's life in one form or another.

Tony did as his mum suggested and found that his visit was to save his bacon as far as Mr Smith's project was concerned. After he had explained to his nan what he was doing, she suggested that he should talk to her husband, someone Tony only knew as Mr Williams. He had never seen Mr Williams outside their flat before, nor had he seen him in anything other than his dressing gown. He was just someone who sat quietly in Nan's front room, reading the newspaper and constantly smoking.

"Go on through and see him," instructed Nan.

Tony did as he was told and went through to see Mr Williams and explain what he wanted. He had never held a long conversation with Mr Williams before and was pleasantly surprised to find him quite lucid in his recollection. It was often said, however, that old soldiers, especially from the Great War and tormented by their memories, rarely talked about everything they had witnessed, and so it was with Mr Williams. He told the young lad about how he had worked in a coal yard that was long since gone; how he had joined the Kennington Pals and done his training up at Catterick; and how he had gone over to France with the Pals and they had fought in the famous Battle of the Somme. He summed up his experience in a few words: mud, rats and the smell of death. A few times during their conversation, he stopped talking and just stared into the middle distance, as if transported back half a century to the unimaginable suffering he and his generation had endured.

Throughout, Tony was scribbling notes down and after about an hour, he could see that Mr Williams was getting tired. Satisfied that he had enough material to keep old Smithy happy, he thanked Mr Williams for his time and made to leave, believing he could now enjoy the rest of his summer holidays. As he was leaving, Nan offered him a carrier bag: "Here, these might help as well, love," she said.

Tony took the bag without checking the contents; he was just happy that he would be able to present a few pages on local history and the First World War when he went back to school. He returned home and enthusiastically told his mum that Mr Williams had been a great help and he could complete his project after all – job done. Without checking the contents, he took the bag Nan had given him and put it in his room, as he had arranged to meet with Mickey and some friends in Kennington Park that afternoon.

It was the following day when Tony decided to write up his notes and put them into some sort of essay that would be acceptable to Mr Smith. After writing six or so pages, he decided that would do the trick. It was only then that he looked in the bag Nan had given him. He was astonished to find what looked like two pairs of war medals and one large bronze disc. Inspecting the medals, Tony saw they were in surprisingly good condition, considering they were so old, and he noticed that they were all inscribed around the rims. He peered closely at each medal: two had "4257 PTE R. Williams 24 London", and two had "46194 PTE L. Williams 24 London". The large bronze disc was inscribed "Reginald Williams" and around the border of the medal was written the words "He died for freedom and honour".

*Wow, that's amazing,* Tony thought to himself and rushed down to show his mum and dad. They agreed and told him to look after them.

"Did the army give you any medals?" Tony asked his dad.

His dad laughed. "No, just a suit that didn't fit, a kick up the arse and the instruction to bugger off!"

"That's not very nice."

"No, but I was one of the lucky ones, some didn't even get a kick up the arse!"

Tony got the impression his dad hadn't particularly enjoyed his war.

"Make sure you give the medals back once you hand your project in," said his mum.

The summer drifted on and instead of forgetting the wretched project that had threatened to ruin his whole holiday, Tony found himself constantly thinking about Mr Williams and the medals. Then, one day during the week prior to the new school term, something suddenly occurred to him that he had never thought of before.

"Mum?" he asked, as she was clearing away the breakfast dishes.

"Mmm," she replied, concentrating more on the task at hand.

"You know Nan?"

"Mmm."

"Well, why is she called Eames and her husband is called Williams?"

His mum stopped as she went to place some dishes in the sink.

"You know, I'm not sure," she said. The question had obviously never occurred to her, either, despite the fact that she had been raised by Nan and had therefore known her all of her life. "I've never given it a thought; we've just always called them Nanny Eames and Mr Williams. I wonder if Eames was her maiden name and it just stayed with her?"

The two remained silent for a few seconds, contemplating the strangeness of it all and the even stranger fact that no one had ever asked the question earlier.

Tony returned to school and handed his project in. He wasn't too surprised to find that old Smithy didn't seem terribly interested in his, or his classmates', summer research. He gave all the projects a cursory glance and handed them back a few days later without indicating any kind of mark. Tony smiled at the irony of it all: at the start of the summer, he had been gloomy at the thought of working on a project that would ruin his holiday; now he was more enthusiastic about it than the history teacher who had given it to him in the first place.

As his task was now complete, he went back round to see his nan with the intention of returning the medals to Mr Williams.

"Can I ask," said the young lad, "why there are two sets of medals?"

Nan and Mr Williams looked at each other.

"I had a brother," said Mr Williams at last, "he was killed when we were in France. So, one set is mine and the other set belongs to my brother, Reg. The large bronze plaque was issued in his memory. All the British soldiers who died during the war received one posthumously. It's known as a death penny."

It was clear to the young lad that Mr Williams was getting upset at the thought of his brother and, therefore, Tony was reluctant to ask further questions, much as he wanted to. Nan seemed to sense the boy's interest and, in an effort to relieve the strange atmosphere, made a suggestion: "There is a box with some old stuff in that might be of interest."

She delved into the bottom cupboard and

brought out an old, battered box. She handed it over to Tony without asking her husband's permission. "You keep this and the medals as long as you like."

As she reached out with the box, Tony couldn't help noticing that she didn't wear a wedding ring. He glanced across to Mr Williams and saw that he didn't either.

"Thank you both so much for your help," he said, sensing now would be a good time to leave.

Mr Williams smiled and waved and Nan saw Tony out.

"Thanks again, Nan, I can't wait to look in the box," he said as they reached the front door.

"That's all right, love, I hope you will find something of interest."

"I didn't realise Mr Williams had a brother."

Nan looked wistful. "Yes, he was such a lovely lad. Everybody loved him. A really lovely lad."

Not for the first time in the last half hour, Tony was seized with a strange feeling that he found difficult to explain.

He rushed home and went straight to his room and opened the box, tipping its contents onto his bed. Out with the contents poured dust and bits that had obviously accumulated in the bottom of the box over decades. Tony wondered how he was going to explain to his mum why his bedspread was now filthy with the grime. *First things first,* he thought.

He sifted through the contents: a few envelopes

– some brown and official looking and two that were small and handwritten – two medical certificates and three photographs. Two were of groups of five and six soldiers, while the third was of two young soldiers on their own. Tony looked at the back, on which was written "Len and Reg, Catterick, July 1916".

*This must be Mr Williams and his brother!*

He turned the photo back over and studied the two young boys – they didn't look much older than he was. They were so alike, they could almost be twins. This was incredible. Tony compared the two lads with the soldiers in the other pictures and clearly saw that each brother appeared in one each, presumably with their other mates from the Pals. There was nothing written on the back of these other photographs.

Tony slumped back on his haunches for a moment, transfixed by the images. These young lads must have still been at their training camp when these pictures were taken. They didn't know what was ahead of them. And poor Mr Williams's brother – and presumably others – wouldn't have known he was never to return home. Tony looked inside the contents of the various envelopes. Inside the brown, official-looking envelopes were forms dated March 1916. They were forms and medical certificates completed when the boys had joined the army. He then opened the two handwritten envelopes: they were letters written from Len Williams to Mary

Eames. *Ah, so Nanny Eames's name is Mary and her husband is Len,* he thought, *that makes sense.*

He felt as though he was somehow invading their privacy by reading the letters but, so engrossed was he in the story, he couldn't help himself. "My dearest Mary" and "Affectionately yours" wrote Len. They were touching without being soppy, and philosophical without being naive. He referred back to Len's army form to check his date of birth: he had been born in 1897. That made him nineteen years old. Tony leaned back again in contemplation. *Wow, that makes him only a few years older than me! I couldn't imagine what it must have been like to write a letter like that, knowing that I was going off to war.*

"Tony! Come and get your tea!"

His thoughts were broken by his mum's call. He bundled everything back into the box, brushed his bed down as best he could and went down to join his mum, dad and sister, Carol, at the dinner table. As his parents chatted about the events of their day, Tony sat quietly, mulling over his own day and the discoveries he had made. This project of Mr Smith's had gripped him and he was determined to find out more about the Williams brothers and their Kennington Pals.

The Death Penny

The Williams' Medals known as The British Medal
also known as Wilfred

The Williams' Medals known as British War Medal
also known as Squeak

CHAPTER

3

# CATTERICK - 1916

"Whose bright idea was this anyway?" asked Reg Williams as he and his brother shovelled away.

"Lord Kitchener, I think," replied Len. "You know – the bloke with the big scary moustache, pointing his finger at us wherever we went. Our country needs us apparently."

"Could have fooled me," moaned the younger boy. "Digging bloody ditches in the middle of nowhere. Hardly helping the war effort, is it."

"Character-building, lad!" announced Len, imitating Sergeant Lawrence who had assured them that the practice would come in handy when they got out onto the Western Front.

"Character-building my ar . . . oh, hello Sarge! We're just digging that trench you asked us to." Reg was suddenly aware of Lawrence, who seemed to appear from nowhere.

"Little less chatter and a bit more digging, lads.

With that, the training sergeant snapped to attention, about-turned and quick-marched away.

"You creep!" said Len to his brother.

"He might give some daft orders but I don't think you would want to cross him," replied Reg, watching the ramrod-straight soldier as he marched away.

"I'm not sure which is harder, this or the coal yard."

The two boys had been working with their dad at Pegg's coal yard when war was declared. It was Kitchener, the Secretary of State for War, who came up with the idea of a volunteer, citizen army of 100,000 men, raised to counter the German numbers that were swarming through mainland Europe. Each man would be between nineteen and thirty years old and would sign up for three years or the duration of the war, whichever was shorter, and would agree to being sent to serve anywhere. The peer pressure made it virtually impossible to ignore the call – within a month of the call going out in August 1914, over half a million men had volunteered.

Len and Reg Williams had not been part of that number, however. There were certain industries that would not allow workers to volunteer on the grounds of their work being of national importance in times of war. The coal industry was one such place of work and, as a result, the boys – and many of their neighbours in Kennington who also worked in the industry – carried on working.

While the volunteers fought abroad, the workers kept the country going back home. Generations had been brought up over the last fifty years with the authorities telling them how great the country was, telling them about the seemingly endless Victorian campaigns where armies left Britain, went off to war in a blaze of pomp and circumstance, and gave the old colonials a good hiding before returning home in glory. Such romantic mythology and over-by-Christmas rhetoric kept everyone's spirits up and created an initial jingoism, buying the government a bit of time during the first few months. But as Christmas came and went, people – fuelled by the press – were starting to question the war: its motives and its cost – both in financial terms and in loss of life – not to mention the length of time it was taking to win the bloody thing.

Funny French place names, like Mons, Marne, Ypres, Neuve Chappelle and Loos were now familiar to the people of Britain. The press were becoming increasingly critical of the tactics on the battlefield and the seemingly crude strategy of continually sending young men over the top to their inevitable fate. After Betty Williams had tried to assist her neighbour Elsie Dorkins – when Elsie had learned of her son's death – she couldn't keep herself from reading the *South London Press*, which carried a story of the battle in which he had been lost. Betty's blood ran cold as she read that young Sydney had been one of 50,000 casualties in that one battle. She thought of her own boys, safe at home working with their father, and wept for Elsie.

Her mood wasn't helped shortly afterwards when the headline screamed, "Conscription Coming".

With thousands of the volunteer army having been lost in battle, the government were forced to introduce the Military Service Bill: for the first time in its history, Britain was introducing compulsory conscription. Every unmarried man and childless widower between eighteen and forty-one was compelled to enlist. When notification came through that that would include eighteen-year-old Reg and his nineteen-year-old brother, Len, their mother Betty burst into tears at the thought of her boys following young Sydney Dorkins. Len was in the same class as Sydney at school and they, Reg and the other boys had all played together on the street and in the park since they were toddlers. Betty thought about those simpler times; not that long ago but they now seemed like a lifetime away. She couldn't help but torture herself with the thought of how many of those young children were destined to suffer the same fate as Sydney. Maybe some of them already had, but Betty just hadn't heard of them. A few months earlier, she had overheard Reg talking to Len about a friend of theirs who had already been killed. She hadn't pressed her son for any details, wanting to know as little as possible about what was happening. But that was before she heard Elsie's shrieking at her loss, and before her own boys received their call to arms. Like everyone else, the war had now come to her own door.

Her fears were shared by young Mary Eames, Len's sweetheart.

Mary's mother, Doris, had been childhood

friends with Betty and as the two grew, married and had children, they remained the best of friends. With Len and Mary being the same age, they were always close and as *they* grew into adulthood, their friendship blossomed into romance. The two had been "seeing one another" – as Len's older sister, Maureen, called it – for nearly two years, and the tension created by the war only brought them closer.

"I'm frightened, Lennie," Mary had told her sweetheart when she learned of the notification. I couldn't bear it if something happened to you, my darling.

"Don't worry, my love," said Len, without a great deal of conviction, "we'll be back before you know it."

It was a characteristically gentle, reassuring comment from Len who had a great empathy with people, especially those who were closest to him. He was as tough as anyone when it came to hard work and standing up for what he thought was right, but at the same time, he had a simple outlook on life. He enjoyed working at the coal yard, close to home alongside his dad and brother. Before the war was declared eighteen months earlier, Len had been dreaming about what the future held. He saw himself as foreman at Pratt's coal yard one day, earning enough money to rent or even buy a small house overlooking Kennington Park. That would be the point at which he could ask for Mary's hand in marriage; they would have a couple of kids, enjoy trips to the south coast as a family and live a simple but happy life.

At the time of the original call to arms – and in order to encourage men to volunteer together – it was thought that many more would enlist if they could serve alongside their friends, relatives and workmates, and so it proved to be the case. Local "Pals" battalions were raised all around the country and associated with their county regiment. When conscription came into being, the initiative was initially maintained and Len and Reg found themselves and their mates from The George waiting to join the Kennington Pals, who would be part of the Queen's London Regiment. With only twenty months between the brothers, they had been virtually inseparable for all of their young lives. Like all young lads, they were full of the bravado of youth, and the sense of camaraderie among them and their mates made the whole thing quite exciting. Despite their mother's fears, there was almost a sense of adventure between the boys – at least it would be different from the back-breaking work in the coal yard.

On the day they joined up in late March 1916, Len and Reg found themselves standing in a queue five deep, which jostled and snaked its way around the streets of South London for three quarters of a mile.

"All sorts, here," said Reg to his brother as he

looked up and down the mass of humanity.

There were bankers, labourers and drunks – some fat, some thin, some tall, some short – men that looked too old and boys that looked too young. Some hadn't followed the original volunteer crowd but were now having their hand forced anyway; many men had been made redundant as industries shed employees in the face of economic uncertainty. For these men, many of whom would soon be hungry, the army at least guaranteed the bare essentials of food, clothing and accommodation. Whether they wanted to or not, conscription was now mopping them all up.

"Look at him," said Reg, pointing to someone a little ahead of them in the noisy line, "he'll never pass the medical. He looks as though he was too old to fight in the Boer War!"

Len laughed at his brother – always the mischievous one. He was never a bad lad but through his demeanour and bravado, he often attracted attention, sometimes even trouble.

Whereas Len was happy with his lot at the coal yard, Reg hated it: ten hours a day, five days a week plus four hours on a Saturday for a pittance of pay. He was always the one who would complain to his foreman, asking why they did a particular task the way they did. Never satisfied with the because-we've-always-done-it-this-way answer, he would get frustrated when his suggestions were ignored, or he was told simply to keep his head down and get on with it. He often looked at his dad, struggling to lift the mercilessly heavy bags, his back virtually broken and his lungs full of dark, vile mucus from years of breathing in coal dust. His dad, like many of the old boys who had been there donkey's years, would regularly cough up a throatful of black phlegm and spit it out onto the greasy cobbles of the yard. Reg often wondered how long it would be before his lungs became as damaged as his dad's. There had to be more to life than this. When he and Len received their call up papers, he gave a wan smile to himself, *be careful what you wish for,* he thought.

"The Germans don't stand a chance," he said to Len, looking up and down the line.

Len followed his brother's gaze. "Are you sure?"

"Not really," said Reg.

The two laughed at their own daftness. Once they got to the front of the queue, they entered a large hall and were faced with three men in khaki, sitting at a trestle table handing out forms.

"Fill this form in," they ordered each man as he came forward, "and take it to the recruiting officer."

"Where's the recruiting officer?" asked Reg.

The three army men all stopped and looked up – it was the first time anyone had asked a question and interrupted their constant, fill-this-form-in-and-take-it-to-the-recruiting-officer script.

"Along there!" barked one, pointing to the far

end of the overcrowded hall where three other men – who, Reg thought, looked exactly the same as these three – sat behind a similar table.

The two Williams boys went over to one of the booths that lined the walls and began to complete Army Form D 418A.

"No going back now," said Len as he signed his form and joined his brother in taking them over to the recruiting officers.

One of the three officers dated and stamped the forms. "These will be sent to the paymaster at the Record Office at your unit," he said. He indicated another door. "Now go through there for your medical."

"Medical?" questioned Reg. "Shouldn't we have the medical before we fill the forms in?"

In a repeat of the earlier incident, all three army personnel stopped and looked up at the new recruit who had dared to question the process.

"Yes, sir," said Len as he bundled his brother towards the open door. He was already beginning to realise that the rule – however ridiculous – was never to question orders. "Keep your big trap shut, Reggie," he said to his brother out of the side of his mouth. "Just do as we're told, I think that's the best way forward."

The two fell in line with the other recruits pouring through the hall into another, similar-sized room that was lined with dozens of chairs, each manned by someone in a white coat. On each chair sat a conscript who was having his ears peered into or his eyes shone with a light, who was being ordered to say "ahh" or was generally being poked and prodded with various instruments. As he vacated his chair, the next man at the front of the endless line was called to take his place.

As they crossed the threshold of the room, the Williams boys were given a form and instructed to give it to the doctor who was to examine them. Both studied the form while standing in the queue. It read:

**A** Able to march, see to shoot, hear well and stand active service conditions anywhere.

**B** Free from serious organic diseases, able to stand service on lines of communication in France, or in garrisons in the tropics.

**C** Free from serious organic diseases, able to stand service in garrisons at home.

**D** Unfit but could be fit within six months.

Beside each letter was a box, presumably in which the doctor indicated the man's suitability for duty. After an examination that lasted less than a minute, the brothers compared their sheets – both had been marked "A1". They joined a further line to hand their sheets in.

"I wonder how many of these are other than A1," commented Reg.

"Not many, I would guess," replied his brother.

By chance, immediately behind them appeared the man Reg had made fun of to his brother by commenting on his appearance and suspected age. Reg nudged Len.

"How did you do, mate?" he asked, addressing the man.

"A1," replied the older man with a thumbs up.

The two brothers looked at each other and smiled.

Within a week, Len and Reg were sent as part of the Kennington Pals to the army barracks in Catterick for basic training.

Despite their natural youth and strength, the lads had to go through the tried and tested sessions that somehow turned civilians into soldiers. Upon arrival, they were greeted by the training sergeants who screeched at them from the moment they climbed down from the rickety old troop vehicles.

"Get in line!"

"Stand up straight!"

"Take that stupid look off your face!"

And so it went on until they were marched to their billet.

Their main instructor, someone they got to know as Sergeant Lawrence, barked out his last order of the day to the bewildered young men: "Your kit is on your bed. Tomorrow morning is as follows:

07.45–08.45 Breakfast in the NAFFI
08.45–10.00 Physical drill
10.00–12.15 Trench training and close-quarter fighting
12.15–13.00 Lunch in the NAFFI
13.00–14.00 Bomb and grenade throwing and the use of machine guns
14.00–15.00 Rifle bayonet fighting – objectives and methods of fire
15.00–16.00 Muscle training with musket – instruction is given in Section 54, para 266 of *Musketry Regulations*."

With that, he tossed a copy of a book – presumably the *Musketry Regulations*, thought Len – onto the nearest bed, about-turned and marched out.

The lads all stood there dumbfounded as to what had just happened.

"What did he say?" asked one, who seemed on the point of tears.

"I don't know," said Reg, "and what's the NAFFI?"

"I'm glad you didn't ask him that," added Len with a sigh. "We'd have probably all ended up in the guardhouse."

The following morning, the two brothers and their comrades found their way to the NAFFI and managed to adhere to the strict timetable as laid out for them by Sergeant Lawrence. The days quickly fell into a regular pattern and as the men became used to their routine and began to grasp the basics of the drills with and without weapons, confidence and anticipation grew among the friends. Reg confided in his brother that he particularly enjoyed the early morning physical drill, "which includes," barked Lawrence on the first day, "rapid individual rushing at fifty yards with fixed bayonets."

When Reg developed an aptitude for this particular exercise, he was inwardly pleased to receive what was to prove a rare compliment from the training sergeant: "You have a talent for that, Williams. It'll come in handy when you're at the front!"

During rifle training, the Pals were trained to fire fifteen rounds per minute.

"This is known as the 'mad minute'! We also use the Vickers machine gun, which has a preloaded ammunition belt of approximately nine yards in length, hence the phrase 'Give them the whole nine yards!'"

Sergeant Lawrence was a career soldier: a veteran of the Boer War, he had also spent the early months of this latest conflict on the Western Front himself. He had been badly wounded and assigned a training post back in Britain to help prepare the civilian army for what they were to face. The Kennington Pals soon learned that when Lawrence spoke, they listened – and listened intently. During one of the briefing sessions, Lawrence showed his recruits some of the less conventional weapons that had been developed by the men in the trenches. One in particular intrigued Private Reg Williams.

"What's that, Sarge?"

"That's a push dagger, lad," replied Sergeant Lawrence, picking it up from the table in front of him. "It was given to me by a Canadian soldier."

From a distance, it looked like something in the shape of a corkscrew, but when Lawrence held it up, the men saw that instead of a screw appendage attached to the grip handle, there was a pointed blade.

"You take the dagger out of its pouch," said the sergeant, demonstrating, "and thrust it forwards, as if you were throwing a punch. Instead, the person on the other end gets four inches of steel inside him for his troubles."

This was all getting very serious and to the point where the young lads from South London were actually looking forward to getting out there. A reality check arrived in early July, however, when they – along with the rest of the country – learned of the bloodiest battle of the bloodiest war so far.

The so-called Somme offensive had been conceived by the British and French and was intended to achieve a decisive victory over the Germans and, in doing so, create a momentum that would see the Allies securing the whole of the Western Front. The reality proved very different from the simple theory. Britain read of 60,000 casualties being sustained on the first day – 20,000 of which were killed. It didn't take long for the Kennington Pals to work out that those men needed replacing, and when they were all handed a booklet entitled, *Hints for Troops in Trenches Handout*, they knew their fate was sealed.

"'Keep feet dry!'" read Reg with a crooked smile to no one in particular. "That's all right then – we've been told."

No one laughed. Everyone just stared at the book in silence. The following week, the men were inoculated against typhoid fever and smallpox, and the inevitable news came through that they would soon be going to France as part of the Expeditionary Force.

As they were leaving camp, Reg picked up a newspaper that had been left in the NAFFI. He gave an ironic laugh. "Here, listen to this, Lennie: 'Because of the success of the Military Act and the subsequent conscription process, there will be no further requirement to form the so-called Pals Battalions.' How lucky are we to be the final Pals?"

"Probably because all the other poor buggers have been wiped out," added Sam Harris, the butcher's lad from Courtney Street.

A few days earlier, one of the lads had arranged for a photographer to visit the camp before they were due to leave. He came into the lads' barrack room, draped a background sheet over a hoarding and placed a seat in front, inviting them to have their pictures taken, some in small groups, some on their own. The Williams brothers had theirs taken together, Len seated and Reg standing over him with his arm around his brother's shoulder.

"Something for Mum and Dad to remember us by!" announced Reg.

His brother looked up at him and shook his head. "You know how to cheer everyone up, don't you?"

On departure day itself, as they were about to leave, Reg summoned up the courage to approach Sergeant Lawrence alone.

"'Ere, Sarge, how much do you want for that push dagger you were showing us?"

"We're not in the business of buying and selling, Williams. We're not market traders!"

"C'mon, Sarge, you know what's in store for us. It's more use to me where I'm going than it is to you."

Lawrence looked at Reg and smiled at his effrontery. He had somehow taken a shine to the young lad and his colleagues and knew there was more of an element of truth in what young Williams said.

"Here you go, lad," he said, taking the leather sheath containing the dagger from his draw. "You're right, there's no charge, but make sure you bring it back," he said with a smile.

The Williams Brothers taken at Catterick Garrison

Catterick Garrison falling out parade

Mary Eames with her mother Doris   picture taken July 1912

CHAPTER

# 4

# LENDERS AND DEBTORS - 1916

Charlie Williams collected his wages on Friday lunchtime as normal. It had been a strange week. There had been no word or revisit from the Connors following his confrontation with Billy the previous Saturday. He assumed that they would be back tomorrow and hopefully just take two weeks' worth of money, probably with a little added on for their inconvenience. He had managed to secure a couple of extra shifts in the week, so he was confident that he could get things back on track, which would not only satisfy the Connors, but keep Betty off his back as well. His two lads were also returning in a few days' time before their deployment, so hopefully they could all enjoy some quiet family time together. Essential to this, of course, was his ability to refrain from his usual Friday night habit of meeting his workmates in The George.

He went straight home, as he had promised Betty, telling his workmates he wouldn't be joining them that night. As he entered the house, Betty and Maureen were giddy with excitement at the thought of seeing Len and Reg again after several weeks away; but at the same time, they found their stomachs were churning with fear due to the boys leaving for France a few days later.

After their meal, no sooner had Betty cleared the dishes from the table than there was a knock at the door. Charlie opened it to find Geordie Wall, one of the lads from work.

"Hello Chas, I know you said you weren't coming down tonight, but the lads have organised a dominoes match and we're a man short. You couldn't spare an hour, could you?"

Charlie looked over his shoulder and back again before dropping his voice. "Geordie, are you trying to get me shot? I promised the wife I would stay in tonight, what with the lads coming in a few days and all."

"Aw, come on Chas, it's only for an hour."

"No, I can't, Geordie."

Betty then came through to see what was going on.

"Hello Betty, love," said Geordie, "I'm just seeing if Charlie can help us out with our dominoes match."

Charlie looked at his wife and shrugged. "I didn't know anything about this, I promise."

Betty returned his shrug and smiled, knowing that Charlie had worked extra hard at the coal yard this week. "Go on then, but just for an hour, mind you."

Charlie grabbed his coat and kissed his wife on the cheek. "Just an hour, I promise." To emphasise the point, he took out his grandfather's watch – his pride and joy – from his waistcoat pocket and checked the time.

Charlie went with his friend to the pub in good spirits. To anyone not used to entering such an establishment, the bar was an assault on the senses. The stink of sweat, beer and tobacco smoke created a heavy atmosphere that caused eyes to sting and made breathing a conscious chore. The toxic air was exacerbated by the almost deafening noise emitted by the dozens of occupants. Used to the atmosphere, Charlie and Geordie didn't flinch on entering The George and seeing their mates sitting at a table, dominoes at the ready.

"Couldn't you find anyone to make the numbers up among this crowd?" asked Charlie, looking round the noisy gathering.

"Ah, we needed a star player, Chas, not just any old arse on a seat," came a voice from the table.

"I can only give you an hour," said Charlie firmly. "I promised the wife I'd be back by half past eight.

"That'll do," said another as the two sat down.

What Charlie Williams didn't know was that he was being watched. The watchers had expected to see their man at his usual Friday night haunt. It just so happened that Charlie wasn't supposed to be here on this night – the fact that he now was, was pure chance. But the mere fact that he *was* here, regardless of the circumstances, was all that mattered to those who were waiting for him.

The game was wrapped up within the hour and

Charlie took out his pocket watch. "Quarter past eight, lads. That's me, I think."

"Can you not stay for another one?" protested one of his friends.

"No," said Charlie, finishing his one and only drink, "I promised Betty, so I will see you later.""

He left his friends, telling them he would see them tomorrow, and went out to make the ten-minute walk back to Queen's Buildings. He had only walked a few yards along Kennington Road when he heard a voice from behind him.

"Hello Charlie."

Charlie turned to see who had spoken to him but as he did so, he felt a fist crash into his face; staggering backwards, he tried to maintain his footing but then another blow from a second thug sent him tumbling onto the road. He managed to get back to his feet but in his dazed confusion, struggled to focus on what was happening. There were now three – or was it even four? – attackers bearing down on him. One swung a punch into Charlie's stomach, doubling him up with a groan; this was followed by someone's knee catching him flush in the face, forcing his nose to explode into a spray of blood.

He managed to connect with a couple of punches of his own but he was no match for the thugs who had numbers and surprise on their side. Blows rained down on him sending him to the floor, while violent kicks to his front and back forced him into semi-consciousness.

“That’s what you get when you don’t pay up. And next time, you should show some more respect!” he heard one of his attackers snarl into his face.

Seeing Charlie’s pocket watch, which had fallen from his pocket during the fight and now hung across his stomach attached by its chain, the thug added, “We’ll just take this as a down payment.” He ripped at the watch, pulling its chain away from the buttonhole which held it. “And don’t think we won’t be back again tomorrow for the rest ’coz we will!”

With that, one of the thugs aimed a final kick at their victim and disappeared into the night. The attack was all over in less than five minutes and Charlie was left bleeding, semi-conscious in the street.

The Kennington Pals arrived back at Waterloo station a few days later. Len and Reg’s mother, their sister, Maureen, and Len’s sweetheart, Mary, were among hundreds of others waiting for their son, brother, sweetheart to return from their training. The atmosphere reflected the mood in the Williams household – excitement mixed in equal measure with trepidation. A cheer went up from the platform as the train came into view, while those aboard waved their caps out of the window. The young men disembarked and were ordered to fall in; the instruction was then given to report to barracks by noon on the following Saturday, when they would prepare for embarkation to France the next day. They then fell out and rushed to find their loved ones.

Len and Reg were smothered with hugs and kisses, and it took them a few minutes to realise someone was missing.

"Where's Dad?" asked Reg.

"Oh, he's at home at the moment," said his mother, "he had a bit of an accident and he's not quite right yet."

"Accident?" repeated Len. "What kind of accident?"

"Oh, something at work, he'll be fine, I'm sure."

The two boys looked at each other, sensing something didn't sound quite right, but had no choice but to accept what their mother was saying. They all made the fifteen-minute walk back to Queen's Buildings, all trying their best to avoid talking about the war and what they were all to face in their own way.

"I'll see you later, Lennie," said Mary, as they came to her door.

The two kissed and Len followed his brother, sister and mother as they headed for their own tenement. The boys simultaneously dropped their kitbags when they saw their father. He was sitting in his chair, his face an angry kaleidoscope of blacks, blues and purples.

"Dad, what the hell happened?" said Len.

"Aw, it was just a stupid accident at work," Charlie

replied with a dismissive wave. “I tripped and fell.”

“Tripped and fell?” exclaimed Reg. “You look as though you’ve been in the ring with Jack Johnson! What happened?”

“Aw it was nothing, I was just filling some coal bags when I got my foot caught in a sack and over I went.”

The two boys looked at each other again, while their mother and sister seemed keen to change the subject.

“Here,” said Maureen, “you two smart lads, let me take your tunics and I’ll hang them up.”

“I’ll get the kettle on,” said Betty, “and we’ll all have a nice cup of tea.”

Reg followed his mother through to the back kitchen. “Mum, what’s going on here?”

“What do you mean?” His mother’s tone was unconvincing.

“Look at the state of Dad. Lennie and me both work at the coal yard – that’s no accident.”

Betty looked down and started to sob.

“Mum, what’s wrong? What’s going on?”

She dried her eyes with her apron, pulled the door to and lowered her voice.

“Don’t say anything to your dad – we both promised him we wouldn’t tell you, but since you boys have been away, times have been even harder than when you were at home. We’ve less money now, so Dad borrowed some from the Connors.”

"Oh no Mum! Not the Connors?" said Reg, knowing what was coming.

"He fell behind with the payments and they took it out on him last Friday night. He had only been to The George for an hour and he was set upon on his way home. He was found lying in the street and one of his mates came round to tell us, they even took his father's watch." That bloody Billy Connor was round here again on Saturday wanting their money."

"Promise me you won't say anything to your dad about this; you know how proud he is. Or your brother for that matter. Promise me," she emphasised to her son.

Reluctantly, Reg agreed to his mother's request as he tried to come to terms with what he was being told. His hatred of the Connors had been building for years. He and Len had gone to the same school as the two Connor boys; he knew what they were like. He saw how they behaved, influenced as they were by their thug of a father. He was still bitter that Billy and Bobby Connor had somehow avoided conscription, while he and Len were going off to fight and who knows if either one of them would return. Things would never change round here unless someone did something about it.

The following few days came and went, with the whole family lost in their own thoughts: the war, the worry, how they would all cope with what the future held.

For *his* part, Reg couldn't get the Connors out of his head; his hatred of them was becoming almost all-consuming. He knew what had happened to Maggie Black and others like her and now this attack on his dad.

The last straw came when he and Len went to visit the wife of their friend who had been killed in the early months of the war, only to learn from a neighbour that she herself was now dead. Like Len and Mary, the couple had been childhood sweethearts and had married at eighteen, just in case the worst happened. When the worst *did* happen and the boys' friend Stephen was killed, his young widow Rose – naïve and unable to cope financially – approached the Connors for a loan. It wasn't long before she found she was unable to keep up the payments and the heartless gangsters responded by adding interest. When she appealed to them to show her some compassion, they responded by first taking most of her valuables including her wedding ring and then when she found she still couldn't keep up with their demands, they suggested another arrangement. This further arrangement lasted three weeks before Rose committed suicide taking a leathal amount of rat poison. She left a note saying she would rather be with her beloved Stephen in the next world, than suffer the horrors of this one. Neither of the couple had reached the age of twenty.

Reg felt his blood boiling as he heard the news. The

Connors had effectively murdered this vulnerable young woman. The police and the Authorities did nothing. Injustice was everywhere and the working man and woman were always the one's to suffer.

Like everybody else, Reg had read about the casualty figures from the front on a daily basis – thousands killed and many thousands more wounded. Would he and Len fare any better when they got over there? And if they both failed to return home, his mum, dad and Maureen would be at the mercy of these bastards. Finally, on the night before they were about to leave – despite his promise to his mum – Reg's mind was made up: he had nothing to lose.

"What are you boys going to do tonight?" asked Betty.

"I'm going to see Mary," said Len, "it'll be the last time for a while and Mary's mum is cooking me dinner."

"I'm going out," said Reg, "probably to The George."

The two brothers left the tenement around eight o'clock and went their separate ways. Len duly headed in the direction of his sweetheart, Mary. Reg, however, didn't go to the pub as he had suggested. Instead, he went to the house of Jack Connor, intent on revenge.

The Connors lived in a house on Kennington Road, much larger than the tenements rented by their persecuted victims. It was well known throughout the area that Jack Connor's wife – tired of the beatings – had left him a few years ago. Jack therefore lived with his two sons in the large house.

Reg stood at the garden gate for a few minutes, contemplating what was about to happen. He had slipped the push dagger – given to him by Sergeant Lawrence on his final day in Catterick – into the breast pocket of his tunic before leaving home. He fingered it reassuringly, before walking up to the door and knocking. It was Jack Connor himself who answered.

"Well, well, well," said the chief thug, smugly, "what do we have here? Come round recruiting, have you?"

Reg was in his uniform – the only decent thing he had to wear.

"I'm Reg Williams."

"I know who you are. And I know your dad, Charlie. How's he doing by the way?"

Reg wanted to knock the smirk off his face there and then but thought better of it, as he had a more permanent solution on his mind.

"Or have you come to pay his debts?" asked Connor.

"Yes, that's it," Reg heard himself say.

"You better come in then," said Connor.

He took him through to the large kitchen at the back of the house. Reg was surprised at the sight of

Connor's shirts hanging on an airer; the London thug was standing in his vest, ironing his own shirts. The heavy hot iron stood on top of the stove waiting to complete its final task – the last shirt that was draped over the ironing board.

"So," said Connor, "what have you got for me?"

"I brought the money we owe you."

"I hope you've got the interest as well," sneered Connor. "Don't think I'm letting you get away with anything just 'coz you come crawling round here."

"I'm not crawling anywhere," said Reg defiantly, his blood boiling hotter with every exchange. As Connor delivered what would be his final insult, Reg saw his father's pocket watch – his pride and joy – on the table. Reg walked slowly towards the table, his back now facing Jack. He was blinded by anger and hatred; he wanted to see this man, this foul bully, crushed and bloodied. He grabbed the handle of the heavy iron that stood on the stove, swung it with all his young might and embedded it into the side of the big man's head.

As the blow struck, Connor's eyes widened into an expression of shock and surprise. He dropped to his knees as Reg let go of the iron, which, through its own weight, dislodged itself and crashed to the floor. Its victim followed a moment later, face first, Connor's already split head hitting the stone floor and exploding into a spray of blood and skull fragments. Reg looked down at the body in front of him: Jack Connor was dead.

Before he could come to terms with what he had done, Reg heard footsteps rushing down the stairs. Moments later, Bobby Connor stood in the doorway trying to comprehend the scene before him. He stood, transfixed by the sight of his father's bloodied body, for what seemed an eternity but could have only been a few seconds before he realised someone else was in the room. Reg Williams was standing there with pure hatred in his eyes.

Bobby Connor looked from Williams to the discarded iron and then to the dark stream of blood that was creeping across the floor from his dead father's head. In a sudden realisation of what had happened, he rushed across the room towards his father's killer.

Reg knew there was no going back now. In the few seconds it took the younger Connor boy to realise what had happened, Reg reached into his breast pocket and pulled the push dagger from its sheath. As Bobby Connor now rushed towards him, he lifted his arm and punched the dagger into his would-be attacker's throat with such force he felt Connor's jaw crunch on the impact of the handle. Blood spurted out of the neck wound as the gagging, twitching Connor stood on tiptoes, impaled at the neck and held in place by the dagger held by Reg Williams. The expression on his face mirrored that of his father minutes earlier.

Reg moved in slowly, until his face was no more than six inches away from Connor's. The dying man's eyeballs moved to look at his killer.

"This is a present from Rose Thomas," snarled Reg Williams, "I'm sure you remember Rose."

He then withdrew the dagger, and the unsupported body slumped to the floor while a fountain of blood spurted from its neck. Reg managed to duck out of the way as the body fell and saved himself from being covered in Bobby's blood.

Reg started to consider his next steps, figuratively and literally. There were pools of blood that were getting bigger by the second and he knew he couldn't afford to step in them. He leaned across and picked up his father's watch. As the blood and bodies were all confined to the kitchen, he knew he had the freedom to wander round the rest of the house unhindered. He checked the soles of his shoes and his uniform and was surprised to find there was no blood at all on the former and very little – considering the carnage – on the latter.

He opened one of the doors from the hallway and found himself in a room that had probably been used by Jack Connor as his office. On the desk were papers and a ledger; he opened the ledger and began to leaf through the pages. There were lists of names and addresses, beside which monitory figures had been written, with various amendments made against some. It was obviously Jack's record of who he had loaned money to and a running total of their repayments. There were hundreds of entries, which could only mean the figures must have run into the thousands.

Reg scanned the room before opening the drawers in the desk. The first thing that greeted him upon opening the top drawer was a handgun. Surprised as he was at the sight, his attitude and approach to handling weaponry was now second nature, following his recent training. He studied the pistol and checked the chamber: it was fully loaded with all six bullets. He laid the gun on the desk and checked the other drawers.

In the large bottom drawer was an equally large strongbox; he heaved it out and dropped it on the desk with a thud. It was locked. He looked in the other drawers and found two keys attached to each other, hidden at the back of the top drawer among several other items. They were identical and were each a perfect match for the box.

Inside the box were bundles of notes. Reg had never seen so much money – it was incredible. He undid one of the elastic bands that was holding each bundle together, and counted out ten five-pound notes. There must have been a dozen such bundles. A thought then occurred to him. He picked up the ledger once more and started to scour the pages until he found what he was looking for: residents of the Queen's Buildings tenements. They were all here on the same page: Elsie Dorkins, Tommy Black, Mr and Mrs Stevens, old Mr David who wasn't fit enough to work anymore. Reg moved his finger down the page and found that virtually everyone in the tenements owed money – or had *paid* money to the Connors – including Charlie Williams.

He slumped back in the chair, trying to make sense of it all. Suddenly, everything was clear: he ripped the page from the ledger and stuffed his pockets with five bundles of notes – *that should cover it*. Locking the box, he replaced it in the bottom drawer and put the keys back in the top drawer where he had found them. His concentration was broken when he heard the front door open.

"All right, Dad? Only me!"

*The other one! Billy Connor!* Reg's thoughts were now very clear: there was no going back, there was no explaining to do and there would be no witnesses. Billy must have sensed something was wrong upon entering the house, as Reg had heard him make no sound from where he was sitting. Presumably, Connor had seen at least one of the bodies lying in the kitchen from where he was standing in the hall. Reg heard him move slowly until he appeared momentarily, passing the room in which Reg was sitting. Billy was clearly trying to take in what he was seeing ahead of him, when his peripheral vision must have registered and he turned back to the study. His eyes fixed on Reg in disbelief.

Reg's eyes were cold, almost unseeing – his hatred of these people was all-consuming. As Billy Connor's expression changed to one of anger and retribution, Reg calmly picked up the gun that was still on the desk and fired: the shot hit Connor in the stomach, sending him backwards until he lost his footing and fell into the hall. Reg walked over and stood over his latest victim, looking him in the eyes without any remorse: "You viciously attacked my dad and said you still wanted the interest payments?" Connor looked up at him with pleading eyes. "Well, Billy, here it is."

Reg raised the pistol and fired point-blank into Connor's forehead.

He was about to leave when he heard a faint sizzling sound behind him. He moved carefully along the hall and leant into the kitchen. The dark slick of blood emanating from Jack Connor's head had found its way to the hot iron that had killed him and which now lay a yard away from his body. The blood was baking on the surface of the iron that had spent the last hour on the top of the stove. The meeting of the two elements was not only creating a soft noise, but it was also filling the air with a vile stench. Reg's pause was only momentary, he felt no remorse. He turned and left, closing the front door behind him. He checked up and down the street to see if anyone was about and walked home.

Maureen was still up when he got back. It was

a warm summer's night, which, coupled with his actions of the last hours, meant Reg was lathered in sweat. He hadn't completely avoided the blood, which spotted his shirt and tunic.

When he came in, Maureen leapt from her chair. "Reg! What's happened?"

"Shh," hissed her younger brother, pointing to their parents' room.

She lowered her voice to a whisper in response but made no effort to disguise her concern. "What happened?" she repeated.

Reg slumped into a seat. "Can you get me a glass of water, sis?"

Maureen hurried through to the kitchen and was back in a moment. Her look prompted her brother again. "I've been round to the Connors'," he said, simply.

"What? Why? What did they do to you?"

Reg half smiled. "They didn't do anything to me. This isn't my blood."

"What have you done?" asked Maureen, still trying to take in the sight of her brother.

Reg turned his head and looked his sister in the eye for the first time. "I killed them, Mo," he said calmly. "I done them all in, once and for all. They won't be bothering us, or anyone else for that matter, ever again."

Maureen stared at Reg in disbelief. "I don't understand. How?"

"It's not important. What they did to Dad last week was the last straw." He took his sister's hand. "I have nothing to lose, Mo. Lennie and me are going away tomorrow and the way things are over there, I don't know if we'll ever be coming back."

"Don't say that."

"It's true. You know it's true – everybody knows it." Reg tried to lessen the tension by adding light-heartedly, "No doubt I'll be killing a few Germans when I'm over there, I was just getting in the mood!"

Maureen didn't laugh. "They'll hang you for this if they find out."

"*If* they find out," repeated Reg, "but they don't have to find out, do they? I'm going away and these animals have been done in. As far as anyone's concerned, the two things are not linked. No one needs to know."

"Apart from me," Maureen protested.

"I'm sorry, Mo, but if I can't trust my big sister, who *can* I trust?"

Maureen smiled at her little brother for the first time. She was tougher than both Len and Reg but couldn't resist either one of them. "Let's get you cleaned up," she said at last, pointing to Reg's uniform.

"There is one other thing," said Reg. He took the bundles of five-pound notes and the page torn from the ledger out of his pocket. "I took these from Connor's study. I thought we could give the money back to the people round here who've been hounded by these thugs."

Maureen looked at the money. "So, you want *me* to give it back?"

"You could just push it through the doors after I've gone."

"Oh yeah, just push it through the doors," said Maureen, pulling a face. "I just have to avoid getting caught, that's all."

"Oh, and one final thing, make sure you give this to Dad if I don't make it back." Reg handed Maureen his dad's watch and smiled.

# CHAPTER

# 5

# ROBERT MCKENZIE

Inspector Robert McKenzie, or "Rab" to his friends – not that he had too many of those – returned to his desk at Scotland Yard after visiting the scene of another attack on a German shopkeeper, this time on Holloway Road.

As the war intensified, anti-German riots were becoming more prevalent; the latest one had been caused when a baker from Düsseldorf, who moved to London six years ago, got into an argument with a customer. The dispute escalated and a riot ensued, with the man having his shop windows broken by a gang wielding bricks and clubs. With resources at a premium, McKenzie and his fellow detective inspectors were having to accompany and supervise their uniformed colleagues in their regular policing duties.

This was the third such riot McKenzie had been called to quell in as many months – this is not what he joined Scotland Yard for, he thought as he sat back down at his desk. He picked up a handwritten note: it was a request to go and see Superintendent Lamb as soon as he arrived. The big Scot exhaled, got up and trudged up the stairs of the large building to the superintendent's office on the fourth floor. He knocked and entered.

"You wanted to see me, sir."

"Ah, McKenzie, come in and take a seat." Clive Lamb's tired face exhibited all the signs of a sixty-year-old man who had been a serving policeman for forty years. "I have a job for you. There has been a series of murders in Kennington."

"Kennington?" exclaimed McKenzie. "That's south of the river."

Lamb had split his detective inspectors into two divisions: one group – which included Rab McKenzie – worked in the north of the capital; one, in the south. As he sat in his superior's office questioning the proposed assignment, McKenzie wondered if the lack of men at Lamb's disposal had forced his hand. Since war broke out, some officers of all ranks had been called up to fight. Although McKenzie himself was a former military man, he chose to remain in his police role.

"Yes, I know where it is," said Lamb, irritably, "but since George Howden's murder, I want someone I can trust looking into it."

Inspector George Howden of the South Division had been found earlier in the year floating down the Thames with a bullet through the forehead. The investigation into his murder had ground to a halt and Lamb had expressed his displeasure with many of his detectives in the South.

"Thank you, sir," said McKenzie.

"It's an unusual case with three people from the

same family murdered in their own home."

"Women and children?" asked the alarmed inspector.

Lamb gave a hollow smile. "Not exactly. A father and two sons – the Connors. Notorious moneylenders, embezzlers and general bullies throughout the Kennington area. Howden had brought them to my attention previously and I've had them down as people of interest in relation to his murder."

"How will the blokes in the South London Division react to me going in there?"

McKenzie wasn't so much questioning his superintendent's decision as reminding his superior of the almost imperceptible conflict between the two groups. At its best, it manifested as good-natured rivalry; at its worst, it led to mistrust and dislike. Everyone knew that Inspector Robert McKenzie was the exception to such nonsense: he was not from London and therefore wasn't interested in any historical territorial ownership. He was only interested in doing his job. Everyone knew it and most gave him a wide berth as a result. The big Scot was his own man who wasn't to be pressured or cajoled by anyone.

Rab McKenzie had ended up in London by way of Carlisle, in Cumberland, and South Africa. Born in the small town of Castle Douglas in the south of Scotland, young Rab was always restless, always wanting to know what was over that hill, who invented that piece of machinery, why so-and-so did such-and-such. He worked on his uncle's farm after his schooling, but it was clear to his family that sooner or later Rab would want to leave the sleepy town to explore what else the world had to offer.

That time came in 1898 when, aged eighteen, Rab crossed the border into England and got a job as a constable in the Carlisle City Police Force. He also joined the local army volunteers that had become part of the Border Regiment a decade earlier. The volunteers would drill, learn about weaponry and attend regular camps. It was never the intention to use them in foreign campaigns but that edict changed with the outbreak of the Boer War in South Africa a year after Rab joined the service.

With heavy losses being suffered, the War Office had announced that it would permit volunteers to join their full-time colleagues on the battlefield and serve one year abroad.

As he now sat in one of his quieter moments, it amused Rab that, less than twenty years later, the whole army virtually consisted of volunteers, given the scale of the current conflict. Back then, in *his* day, the strict criteria had been that each man would have to be between the ages of nineteen and twenty-five, should be passed medically fit for action by army personnel, should be a first-class marksman and should, preferably, be unmarried. Rab fit the bill perfectly – within eighteen months of his joining what was thought to be a semi-social group of part-time soldiers, he had been travelling halfway around the world to fight a war he knew little about. *How little has changed,* he thought as the current conflict raged on.

So there he had been as the new century dawned – the great adventurer preparing to sail off to war. What he and his colleagues would encounter was twelve months of long marches across the high South African veldt and fierce fighting with Boer Kommandos.

Within a year of the conflict erupting, it had descended into barbarism: the Boers skilled in hit-and-run guerilla tactics, the British merciless in burning Boer villages and housing women and children in concentration camps. By the time the volunteers' statutory twelve months' service was completed, the conflict was still raging and showed no signs of ending.

Although it was a challenging twelve months for the young Scot, Rab McKenzie felt there was still work he could be doing – it felt far too early for him to be returning home. With his colleagues preparing to leave Cape Town in April 1901, he made enquiries about joining the South African Constabulary, or SAC as it was known among the men. The SAC was a paramilitary force set up the previous year to keep the peace in British-controlled areas, but as the

Boer resistance continued, its four divisions instantly became involved in military, rather than policing, duties.

Finally, in the latter half of 1901, the British began to gain ascendency in the war due to the sheer weight of numbers of men from around the Empire, and by early 1902 even the most stubborn of Boer Kommandos were beginning to realise that continued resistance was futile. In May of that year, the Boers agreed to surrender their independence to the British and recognise the authority of King Edward VII.

Once hostilities were over, the regular soldiers followed their volunteer colleagues home and each SAC division began to undertake the duties it had originally been established for. Rab McKenzie remained in South Africa for a further six years, during which time the SAC was gradually reduced until it was disbanded altogether in 1908. While some of its members chose to make South Africa their permanent home, others returned to the various corners of the Empire from whence they came. Rab, however, was at a loss as to what he should do: there was little for him back in Carlisle and – with his parents now dead and with no opportunity to carry out any form of police work in Castle Douglas – there was even less in his home town.

During his eight-year career with the SAC, he had worked alongside colleagues from Australia,

Canada and Ceylon. He wondered if there may be opportunities for him in those colonies but gravitated back to a suggestion made to him a couple of years earlier by George Davis – a chap ten years Rab's senior – from London, who had mirrored Rab's journey from a uniformed constable to army volunteer. Rab and George knew each other a little during their army service but then became good friends as part of the SAC. George left the SAC a couple of years before its disbandment and informed Rab about the opportunities back home in the Scotland Yard Detective Division. He told the Scot that if he was ever interested in following his lead, he should get in touch and George would see what he could do for him.

With the SAC no more, and Rab a little unsure as to how he would be viewed and treated by the re-empowered locals, he felt it was a good time to go. He contacted Davis in London, who put in a good word for his old friend. McKenzie had sailed back to England and attended an interview before securing a position as a detective sergeant. Within two years, he had advanced to inspector and by the outbreak of the Great War was considered by Superintendent Lamb to be his best man in the North Division. The only time Rab travelled south of the river these days was to visit his old friend George from South Africa, who had retired from the Yard eighteen months earlier.

"The 'South London blokes', as you so ably put

it," said Lamb in response to McKenzie's question, "will have to answer to me. If anyone has any issues with my decision-making, I am more than happy to discuss it."

"Yes, sir," replied the inspector, not particularly bothered himself what anyone's reaction might be. "When did the murders take place?"

"Sometime over the weekend. They were found this morning, when" – Lamb hesitated for effect – "a friend of the family, apparently, reported finding the bodies in the back kitchen of their house on Kennington Road."

"And presumably this . . . friend of the family . . . was anonymous and cannot be traced?"

"Brilliant deduction, Inspector."

The two policemen exchanged knowing smiles.

"Go down to the second floor," instructed the senior man, "and gather what information is available. Then visit the scene and report back your findings by close of play tomorrow."

"Yes, sir."

The South Division were housed predominantly on the second floor of the Scotland Yard building, while McKenzie and his colleagues north of the river occupied the third. Rab McKenzie therefore followed Superintendent Lamb's instruction and visited his colleagues on the lower floor.

As he entered the room, there was a noticeable lowering of voices, almost to the point of silence.

Not that any of that bothered the Scot; throughout his adult life he had felt like an outsider: in an English regiment in the army, as a police officer in South Africa, and now – despite his years of service in London – as an interloper in the nepotistic environment of Scotland Yard. He approached Sergeant Jim Mortimer, who was responsible for signing in the various cases as they were brought to the attention of the division.

"Can I have the Kennington papers, please, Sergeant?"

"Which Kennington papers might those be, Inspector? We currently have six cases ongoing."

McKenzie couldn't be sure if Mortimer was being efficient or just awkward. He decided to give him the benefit of the doubt. "The three murders that apparently occurred over the weekend," he clarified.

"Certainly," said the sergeant, handing the inspector a single piece of paper.

McKenzie took it and read: "'Three murders took place on Kennington Road, possibly on Friday or Saturday night. Reported anonymously.' Is that it? Superintendent Lamb told me that already."

"That's all we've got, I'm afraid. Probably a burglary gone wrong or a neighbouring gang taking some sort of revenge."

The benefit of doubt McKenzie had originally afforded Mortimer was starting to dissipate. "Have there been previous dealings with these Connors?"

The large writing room was now completely silent as its occupants listened to the exchange. Someone tried to suppress a laugh and gave an involuntary snort at McKenzie's question. The Scot turned his head slightly at the sound, barely moving, then turned back to Mortimer and said, "Well?"

"I think they have crossed our paths once or twice," Mortimer said with a slightly smug air.

"Give me the other Kennington cases you referred to."

"I thought you were just looking into the murders?"

McKenzie's patience had now worn out; he leaned over the desk and had to refrain from grabbing the sergeant by his lapels. "Are you questioning my authority, son?"

Mortimer's eyes widened as he realised he had overplayed his hand. "Sorry, sir, yes, they're right here," he spluttered, sifting through the pile of files and handing over the five he had referred to.

By this point, the atmosphere in the room had changed from one of smug amusement to one of heads-down-and-mind-my-own-business.

McKenzie flicked through the files before tossing three back onto Mortimer's desk. "These two," he said, holding the others, "one refers to an embezzlement case and the other to a severe beating and robbery that took place near the Lambeth Walk a week ago. The Connors' names appear in them. Who were they assigned to?"

"Erm, Inspector Reeves, I think, sir," spluttered Mortimer.

McKenzie turned to face the room as he asked, "And where is he?"

"He's away at the moment, sir. Off on sick leave."

"Right," said the big Scot, "I'm taking these two files with me and tell him when he gets back that I would like to see him. Is that clear?"

"Yes, sir, perfectly clear." In an effort to regain a little credibility, Mortimer added, "I believe there is a pathologist down there at the scene of the murders right now, Inspector."

Rab McKenzie ignored the comment and marched out of the silent room, partly appalled that so-called colleagues would behave in such a manner, and partly having quite enjoyed the exchange.

Inspector Robert (Rab) Mackenzie

Murder Weapon Number 1

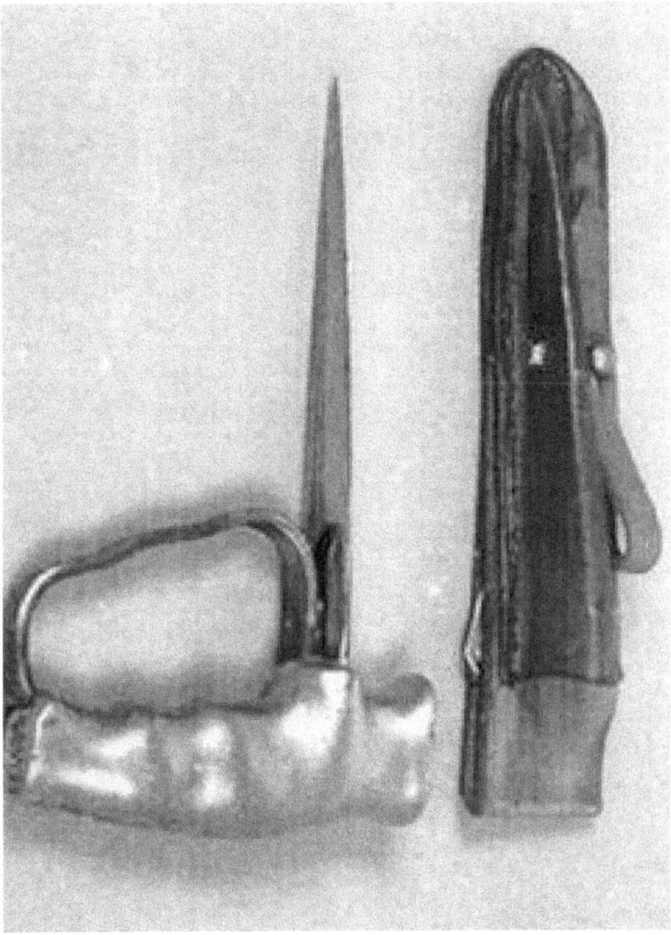

Murder Weapon Number 2
Canadian Push Dagger

Murder Weapon Number Three
Police Issue Webley Pistol

# CHAPTER 6

# THE INVESTIGATION CONTINUES - 1970

As the new term progressed, Tony took and passed his mock exams, still not really sure what he wanted to do when he left school in less than a year's time. Instead, he found his mind increasingly occupied by Nan's husband, Len, and his brother, Reg. He wasn't sure why, it was just something that had captured his imagination. What's more, he somehow felt there was more to the story than he knew; he wasn't sure what it was but there was something about Mary Eames and Len Williams that didn't seem quite right.

When he was telling his dad about the contents of the box, his dad replied that many old soldiers, especially from the First World War, don't like being reminded of their war time experiences.

"As a result, there are always gaps in people's stories and recollections."

*Maybe that was it,* Tony thought – just a case of people's memories being clouded after so many years.

As the nights drew in and the clocks went back, Tony spent more and more time in his room reading and rereading the letters and documents given to him by his nan. He was also fascinated by the photographs of the young soldiers. Looking into their eager, enthusiastic eyes, it seemed they had no idea – when the pictures were taken – as to what lay ahead for them. Tony felt a sadness for them, as he knew something they didn't – some of them would never return. Among them would be Mr Williams's brother.

He studied the picture of the two boys; which one was which? Each one also appeared separately in other pictures, taken with groups of the other recruits. In one, they were all holding their rifles and smiling; Tony imagined the banter that was taking place as the picture was being taken: chatter about how the Germans didn't stand a chance and what they were going to do to them. In the particular picture Tony was studying, the Williams brother – whichever one it was – held the butt of his rifle in the crook of his left elbow. He compared the picture with the image of him and his brother but struggled to identify which was which. It was fascinating stuff but he was itching to find out more.

On the Saturday morning before the half-term holiday, Tony's mum sent him out for some milk and a few vegetables from the shops. "Call in and see if your nan wants anything on your way," she instructed, knowing that he would have to pass her house.

Far from being annoyed by the task given to him by his mother, Tony was delighted, as it gave him another opportunity to go and see his nan, and if he could steer the conversation round to his wartime research involving Mr Williams and his brother, then all the better.

Armed with the list given to him by his mum, he hurried off in the direction of his nan's.

"Hello, love!" exclaimed Nan as she opened the door. "What brings you here?"

"Mum's sending me down the shops and asked me to call in and see if you needed anything."

"Aw, that's a lovely thought. I don't think I need anything but no doubt his nibs" – she threw her head back in the direction of the living room – "will want something. Come on in, love, he's just on the telephone to an old friend of his."

Tony was surprised to learn that Mr Williams had any friends; he'd never seen him outside the house before and wasn't aware of any other visitors. He followed his nan through to the living room, however, just as he was putting down the telephone. He was sitting in his usual chair, in his usual dressing gown.

"Young Tony here wondered if you wanted anything from the shop," she announced.

"Aw, you're a good boy," said Mr Williams at the sight of the lad, "I could do with some Capstans." He gestured to his wife. "Get my wallet out the bottom drawer, Mary. And maybe a packet of them glacier mints – my throat's been playing up again and they help a bit ."

Unprompted, Mr Williams took a pen and pad that lay beside his newspaper and wrote down the few items. "There you go, son, just in case you forget."

"I'll have a nice glass of dandelion and burdock waiting for you when you get back," said Nan.

"Thank you," said Tony. Like most kids his age, he could never work out whether he actually *liked* dandelion and burdock or not, but it was a good reason to return and hopefully ask a few more questions, so he made sure he sounded enthusiastic.

He went to the shops, trying to work out what he wanted to ask Mr Williams when he returned. His mind wasn't particularly on the task he had been given, but he did have the presence of mind to continually refer to both the list given to him by his mother and the one given to him by Mr Williams, making sure that nothing was missed. He was back at his nan's house within twenty minutes.

"There you go, Tony," she said, sitting him down and giving him the glass of pop. "Now, tell us what you have been up to."

Tony's mum had once told him that Mr Williams had a sister, but apart from that he knew they didn't get much company, so no doubt they were as pleased to see him as he was to see them.

"Oh, just school stuff, you know?"

"Yes, it'll be your exams this year, won't it?"

"Yes, that's right. I had my mock exams a few weeks ago and they went really well so I'm hoping things should be OK by the time I get to the real thing next summer."

"What are your subjects?" asked Mr Williams.

Now was his chance.

"Well, I'm doing a few things and I'm really enjoying studying history."

"In fact, the project that you helped me with was great. It really went down well with Mr Smith, our history teacher."

*A little white lie here and there won't hurt anyone,* he thought.

"That's nice"

Nan was neither dismissive nor encouraging with her response, so Tony pressed on.

"I wondered if you could tell me a little bit more about your brother and the Kennington Pals, Mr Williams."

Mary and Len exchanged a look that, once again, confused Tony.

"It was a long time ago, son," said Mr Williams at last, "I'm not sure I could remember much about it."

He attempted to clear his throat and something that initially sounded like a tickly cough gradually escalated into a coughing fit that saw him struggling for breath. Nan got up and went over to help by patting him on the back, but it took a good thirty seconds for him to settle down.

"He's been like this for over a week now," Nan

said to no one in particular.

Tony sat there, feeling guilty, and it looked as though he was going to be denied the thing he was particularly interested in. Despite his eagerness to know more, looking at Mr Williams he recognised it would be difficult to continue with his questions, so he stayed a little while longer before making his excuses to leave.

"I better get these groceries home to Mum before the milk goes off," he said with a smile

"Yes, that's a good idea, love," said Nan, "and thanks again for running that errand for us."

"No problem. Hope you're feeling better soon, Mr Williams," he said as he followed his nan to the front door.

"I won't, son, believe me," murmured Mr Williams with a wave as he leaned back in his chair, still trying to regulate his breathing.

"Where have you been?" asked his mum when he returned. "I was just about to send out a search party."

"Oh, I just called in at Nan's with the shopping she wanted. She gave me a glass of pop."

"How are they doing?"

"Nan is OK but Mr Williams is not very well. He's got a terrible cough that he can't get rid of."

"There's a good reason for that cough, did he not mention it?" his mum said. "He was caught in a gas attack while fighting in France; many of his friends died. Len survived but has suffered with serious lung problems ever since. In a strange way, being gassed probably saved his life, as he came back to England for hospital treatment and never went back to fight in France again. I'll go round and see them tomorrow, to see if there's anything I can do."

While his mum was round at his nan's, Tony spent most of the morning in his room, looking over the contents of Mr Williams's box for the umpteenth time. His dad was downstairs reading the paper, while his sister, Carol, was playing with a friend nearby. His mum returned at about eleven o'clock to start preparing the Sunday dinner. When he heard the front door, Tony went downstairs – as casually as he could – to see if there was any news from Nan's. In truth, of course, he selfishly wanted to know if it would be OK for him to go round and speak to Mr Williams.

"He's not right," he heard his mum telling his dad as he entered the living room.

"Mr Williams?" Tony questioned.

"Yes," replied his mum, "he has a terrible chesty cough and his breathing is getting worse. I told Nan to call the doctor tomorrow. Anyway, I'll get on with the dinner."

"I'll give you a hand with the vegetables, if you like," said Tony.

His mum looked at him and his dad flopped the paper into his lap.

"*What?*"

"I . . . I just thought you might want a hand, that's all."

"First time for everything, I suppose," said his mum, "follow me."

His dad just shook his head and went back to reading his paper.

Tony had been helping for about ten minutes when he plucked up the courage to broach the one subject that was dominating his thoughts these days.

"Mum? Do you think Mr Williams is going to be all right?"

His mum was flitting about the kitchen, doing several tasks simultaneously, as only mums can do.

"I don't know, love. He's not well and hasn't been for years, but now it seems to be getting worse."

"Mmm," replied Tony as he attempted to direct the conversation, "I sometimes feel a bit sorry for him and Nan. They don't seem to have any family."

Tony's mum stopped what she was doing and thought about Tony's observation. "No, I don't suppose they do. I know Nan had a baby when she was a young woman, it was a girl but I believe she died when she was an infant. It must have been terribly painful for her and I've never asked her about it. The only link to the past that is left is Mr Williams's sister, Maureen. I have met her a couple of times and she is really nice."

"I was thinking about going round again to see

him to ask about his brother and the war," said Tony.

"I thought you'd finished that. Wasn't it a project for Mr Smith?"

"Well, yes, it was, but I think it's so interesting that I'd like to know a little bit more. Have you seen the picture Nan gave me of Mr Williams and his brother?

"They were very much alike, not identical but very similar. His brother Reg was killed in the war but I'm not sure when, where or how."

"I think it would be best to leave him alone for a little bit, love. It's not the time to be bothering him with that sort of thing."

"I suppose so," said Tony, knowing his mother was right.

He finished his task and wandered back through to the living room.

"What's up?" asked his dad over the top of his newspaper.

He repeated what he had said to his mum about Mr Williams and his brother.

"What was the regiment again?"

"They were in the Kennington Pals, which was part of the London Regiment," said Tony.

"Well, while Mr Williams is out of action, why don't you go down to the library? They're bound to have some information there. No doubt they'll have back copies of the local newspapers – you'll be able to trawl through them and see if you can find out a bit more information."

"What a brilliant idea, you're a genius! I never thought of that. Thanks, Dad."

"Yes, I am, so don't forget that," Tony's dad replied, going back to his newspaper.

Tony scampered off to his room and engrossed himself once again in the contents of the box for an hour or more. And now, thanks to his dad's suggestion, he could go to the library on Monday to see if he could find out anything further without bothering Mr Williams.

"Dinner's ready!" he heard his mum call.

Downstairs, his sister had returned and she and their dad were going through to the kitchen as the food was being dished out.

"Where is that boy?" his mum asked.

Tony's dad went to the bottom of the stairs. "Oi, Sherlock Holmes, come and get your dinner!"

Like an infuriating crossword puzzle that was almost finished, Tony took another look at the material before him and decided that he would have to wait until Monday before he could make some meaningful progress in finding out more about 4257 Private R Williams and 46194 Private L Williams of the 24th London Regiment.

# CHAPTER

# 7

# THE INVESTIGATION COMMENCES - 1916

As the police vehicle carrying Inspector McKenzie trundled round the corner onto Kennington Road, it was obvious to him and anyone else in the vicinity where the crime had taken place. Down the street, a crowd had gathered around the house in question. An ambulance was parked outside, while three uniformed officers were attempting to marshal the onlookers and guard the scene of the crime at the same time.

The police vehicle pulled up as close to the house as it could. The three officers turned to see which inspector had been sent to the scene. As McKenzie climbed out, their faces assumed the same expression of surprise.

"Inspector," said one of the policemen, "we weren't expec—"

"It doesn't matter who you were expecting, Constable," interrupted McKenzie, "now get these people away from here."

He walked through the group of around twenty people towards the front door, which was ajar.

"Yes, sir," said the bobby after him, adding – in an effort to gain some credibility – Dr Spilsbury is in there now."

McKenzie pushed the door open carefully,

unsure as to what he was going to see inside. What he did see was the police pathologist kneeling over a body that was lying in the hallway.

"Hello, Bernard," said McKenzie.

The pathologist looked up. "Rab! I never expected to see you here. You do know we're south of the Thames, don't you?"

"Yes, I believe so," said the inspector with a smile. Superintendent Lamb asked me to take charge of the case."

The cordial exchange between the two reflected a mutually appreciative working relationship enjoyed for some time. Bernard Spilsbury had been working as a pathologist for Scotland Yard for many years before Rab McKenzie joined the force. Whenever the two worked together, they each appreciated the other's skills. There was no jealousy, no trying to put each other down, just a mutual respect that suited both men who simply wanted to do their respective jobs as well as they could. Spilsbury had retired two years earlier but when war was declared and resources became depleted, the Yard contacted him and asked if he would return to his duties as and when required. Now was just such a time.

"So, how have you been, Bernard?" asked McKenzie. "Still enjoying your retirement?"

Spilsbury looked from McKenzie to the body beneath him and back again. "Oh, yes," he said with a crooked smile, "loving every minute of it."

It was a back-and-forth Rab McKenzie would have exchanged with very few people, which suggested that Dr Spilsbury could almost be described as a friend – or as close to a friend as the Scot had.

"So, what do we have here?" asked the inspector, getting down to business.

"A bit of a mess, I'm afraid," said Spilsbury, getting to his feet. He was wearing some overalls and McKenzie noticed dark bloodstains on the knees.

"Three deaths, this one here and two in the kitchen," Spilsbury indicated over his shoulder. "What is interesting is that each one has suffered a different death. This one here appears to have been shot twice, once in the stomach and then fatally, almost point-blank, through the forehead; the other younger victim has a puncture wound to the neck, as though he has been garrotted, and the older victim appears to have received a violent blow, again directly to the side of head. There's a clothes iron caked in dry blood lying near the body – the chances are that was the object that was used."

McKenzie contemplated the macabre scene. He eased past Spilsbury and leaned through the kitchen entrance without entering and unnecessarily disturbing the scene. Congealed pools of blood virtually covered the stone floor; Dr Spilsbury's footprints were visible from where he had unavoidably padded across the floor to carry out his initial inspection.

"When did you arrive?" asked McKenzie.

"I've been here for about an hour."

"Were there any other signs of footprints?"

"No, that struck me as strange. There is so much blood, I thought the killer would have had to trail through it. Unless they killed each other, perhaps."

"For that to happen," McKenzie thought aloud in response to the pathologist's observation, "one of them must have shot this one in the hall and then a fight ensued in the kitchen. They would then have had to administer their fatal blows almost simultaneously. Highly unlikely, I would have thought – and besides, they were members of the same family, what would they be fighting about?"

"Yes. Anyway, with your permission, Rab, I'll get these bodies removed and carry out a full autopsy. I'll have my reports with you hopefully by tomorrow."

"That's fine, Bernard, thank you."

Dr Spilsbury's two orderlies had been waiting patiently in the ambulance all this time; finally, the pathologist called them inside and asked them to remove the deceased.

As the bodies were being carried out, McKenzie entered the study, partly to get out of the way of the delicate operation and partly to see if there was anything he could find that would assist him in his investigation. He heard muffled cheers from the dispersing crowd outside and went to the window to see what the disturbance was. Most of the people that were still on the street appeared to be voicing their approval at the Connor family's demise. Two newspaper men had arrived on the scene and as one of the covered stretchers was being loaded into the ambulance, one was taking a photograph. *Interesting,* thought the policeman as he turned his attention back to the room before him.

On the desk was a pile of papers, on top of which sat a ledger. McKenzie picked up the book and flicked through the pages, observing the lists of names and addresses it contained. They meant nothing to him but it was clear by the figures beside each name that they were Connor's records of monies loaned and repaid. He was about to put the ledger down when he noticed, between two pages, some straggly fragments of paper were protruding from the binding – a page had been torn out. McKenzie contemplated the significance of this discovery for a few moments before inspecting the contents of the drawers.

The top drawer housed an assortment of pens and pieces of paper – nothing apparently of any significance. The larger bottom drawer contained a locked strongbox; McKenzie removed it, gave it a slight shake to discover something was inside and placed it on the desk. He knew it was futile to check the bottom drawer for the keys but he did it anyway as a matter of course. He then turned his attention back to the top drawer and emptied the contents onto the desk. At the back of the drawer, he found exactly what he was looking for: two small keys that fit the lock of the strongbox. Contained within were hundreds of pounds in bundles of notes. *If there was a fourth person in the house, the motive could not have been burglary,* he thought.

The three uniformed officers were still guarding the premises, so McKenzie called two of them inside. "What are your names?" he asked.

"Geddes and Beattie, sir," said one, indicating which one was which.

"Are you both local lads?"

"Yes, sir."

He handed Geddes the ledger. "Have a look through this book and tell me if you recognise the streets named."

Constable Geddes did as he was instructed and glanced through the pages for a few moments. "Yes, sir, they look as though they are all streets in the Kennington area."

"And these Connors – known to us, were they?"

The two policemen looked at one another, uncertain as to what they should say for fear of somehow incriminating themselves or their colleagues.

"Come on," commanded McKenzie, "I'm not interested in stupid schoolboy pacts of silence! What's past is past, we can't change it. But whatever we think of these people, we are obliged to investigate their murders. If we don't, there would be a free-for-all and it would lead to anarchy."

Suitably assured, Geddes replied, "Well, yes, sir. They were the local bullies in the area, moneylenders, black marketeers, robbers. If there was any trouble round here, it invariably involved the Connors in some way; however, we just could not get the evidence to convict them, no one would come forward."

Since the outbreak of the war, there were families and gangs in every borough of the city who had taken advantage of the emergency situation. McKenzie referenced this point: "Was there ever any suggestion of rival gangs infringing on their area, or vice versa?"

The two constables looked at each other with not-that-I-know-of expressions.

"Don't think so, sir," said Geddes.

"So, the chances are, it's someone who has taken their revenge on these people." McKenzie was talking to himself as much as to his uniformed colleagues.

"But they're just ordinary people round here, sir," said Beattie, "I don't think they would have the nerve or the skills to break into the Connors' house and murder the three of them."

"No," agreed the inspector, "so whoever it was, they were fit and able to handle a knife and a gun and were willing to kill." He referred to the ledger that Geddes was still holding. "In that book, there is a page that has been torn out. I want you to go through it – by process of elimination, we should be able to identify which addresses have been removed.

"Beattie, I want you to take an inventory of everything in the house."

Beattie momentarily considered protesting, given the enormity of the task, but quickly decided that McKenzie was not a man to be disobeyed. "Yes, sir," he said, almost under his breath.

"Report back to me this afternoon. And remove that iron from the kitchen for further examination."

The constables gave a collective "Yes, sir" as the inspector walked out.

Outside the house, the newspaper man on the other side of the street shouted across to the policeman, "Any idea who was behind it, Inspector?"

McKenzie ignored the question and made his way back to the station where he went straight up to see Superintendent Lamb, who was impressed at the progress made by McKenzie in such a short period of time. "What are your next steps?" he asked.

"I am trying to identify the addresses on the missing page of Connor's ledger," replied McKenzie. "I hope to get some idea later this afternoon. If I do, I'll be starting some door-knocking tomorrow."

"Good work, McKenzie. Report back to me tomorrow afternoon."

"Very good, sir."

It was mid-afternoon when constables Geddes and Beattie knocked on the door of McKenzie's office. "Here is the inventory you asked for, sir," said the latter.

"And the addresses?" he asked Geddes.

"By my reckoning, sir, the only addresses I can't account for within the pages of the book are those in Queen's Buildings, not far from the Kennington Road."

"Right, I suggest that's where we start our enquiries, gentlemen."

"Who was the other constable with you this morning?"

"Donnelly, sir," said Geddes.

"Right, I want you two and Donnelly to carry out some door-knocking at these Queen's Buildings. Let's see what you can find out and report back here at twelve o'clock tomorrow lunchtime."

CHAPTER

# 8

# THE INVESTIGATION CONTINUES

Bernard Spilsbury knocked and entered McKenzie's office at ten o'clock the following morning.

"Hello, Bernard, I wasn't expecting you until this afternoon," said Rab, pleasantly surprised.

"Well, I knew you wanted the information as quickly as possible, so I worked late last night and was in early this morning."

"That's good of you, thanks."

Spilsbury handed over a file. "These are the full reports on the three autopsies."

McKenzie opened it and spoke as he read. "So, did you find anything out of the ordinary?"

"You mean, apart from the one corpse with an iron embedded in his skull, another one with his throat lacerated and the third with bullet wounds to his stomach and head?"

McKenzie smiled at the stupidity of his own question. "Let me put it another way. If there was nothing wrong with the two younger victims, why wouldn't they have been conscripted into the army like everyone else? The way things are right now, if you've got two arms and two legs, you get in."

"The thought did cross my mind as I was studying the bodies," Spilsbury concurred. "I have to say, Rab, that if you are having doubts about some colleagues in your profession and their relationship with these people, then I am having similar concerns about some colleagues in mine. These young men would have been fit enough for conscription, so it appears as though someone in authority has some questions to answer as to why they were overlooked.

"That said, there were no differences in the conditions of the bodies – that is to say, I would estimate they died around the same time. Between two and three days ago."

"I would agree with your suggestion that the iron was used as a murder weapon," McKenzie said, pointing to the object that was standing up on a bureau to the side of his desk. "There are fragments of blood on the point."

"Yes," said the pathologist, going over and picking it up, "the initial wound to the side of the head is consistent with the pointed end of the iron. It was wielded with such force that I found skull fragments in the brain. The impact sent the body into cardiac arrest and he fell forwards, smashing his face on the stone floor. Death would have occurred in a matter of seconds, if not instantaneously."

He returned to his seat. "It's the victim with the neck wound that interests me. I can't be sure what the weapon was that was used, but whatever it was, it was plunged straight into the neck on the victim's left side with such severity, the victim's jaw broke.

It's as if there was a handle or a secondary weapon attached to the blade. The blade itself severed the carotid artery – the victim would have bled to death in a few minutes."

"The left side of the victim?" questioned the policeman. "So, that suggests the killer was right-handed. He was also an expert in what he was doing, or he got very lucky."

"Whoever it was he must have had quite a nerve to enter the house and commit three different murders consecutively."

McKenzie thought for a while. "There is no sign of a break-in and clearly burglary wasn't the motive. So, the killer was known to the victims and was invited in. I'm beginning to think there was an argument and the matter escalated. Why would the killer use the iron when he had access to a gun and some sort of knife?"

"Maybe he didn't have a gun. Maybe he discovered it in the house. It's worth noting, incidentally, that the bullets extracted from the victim in the hall were from a Webley pistol – the same gun type and model that killed Inspector George Howden earlier this year. Could be coincidence of course. Either way, this is where I have to hand it over to you, Rab."

"Of course. Thank you for your help, Bernard."

The two shook hands and the pathologist left the policeman to his enquiries.

On the stroke of twelve o'clock, constables

Geddes, Beattie and Donnelly returned with their morning's findings.

"Well, gentlemen," said McKenzie, "what did you uncover?"

Geddes acted as spokesman. "Well, sir, between us we covered all but three addresses in the Queen's Buildings. Our overriding feeling is that most people knew of the Connors' murders, whether that was because the bodies were found only yesterday or they knew beforehand, we couldn't tell. No one was letting on how they heard the news – it was all 'somebody said' or 'I heard something about it'. What was clear is that they all seemed pleased."

"So, they had all had dealings with the Connors at one time or another?"

"It seems so, sir. Times are hard, I suppose. With most of the young men being away, income is scarce. It's almost inevitable that they have been borrowing money."

"You said there were three addresses you didn't get a reply from?"

"Yes, sir" – Geddes referred to his own notebook and then to Donnelly's – "numbers 5, 17 and 24. We asked at the neighbours of each; apparently at number 5 are a Charlie and Betty Williams, number 17 is a Mrs McAteer, and number 24 is a George Quinn. We can go back this afternoon if you like and see if we can catch them in?"

Inspector McKenzie thought for a while. "Charlie

Williams?" he said at last, sifting through some files on his desk. "That name rings a bell. Ah, here we go. There was a Charlie Williams beaten up and robbed of his pocket watch after leaving The George pub in Kennington a couple of weeks ago."

"Could be coincidence, sir," suggested Geddes.

"Mmm, could be," McKenzie thought aloud, "but I don't like coincidences. And I don't believe in them, either."

"Would you like us to go back this afternoon, sir?"

McKenzie paused again, his mind trying to unpick the information he and his men had gathered. "No, I think I'll go back myself. That will be all for the time being. Put yourselves on standby and I'll let you know the next steps."

"Very good, sir," said Geddes.

Rab went to see the superintendent to update him on the latest position. Both he and his superior officer were becoming increasingly intrigued by the investigation. The world was certainly a better place without the likes of the Connors, yet a serious crime had been committed.

"What do you propose next?" asked Lamb.

"I will go and visit these last three inhabitants of the Queen's Buildings myself, sir," replied McKenzie.

Superintendent Lamb nodded slowly. "Very well, carry on and keep me updated."

It was another lovely summer's afternoon as

Rab McKenzie arrived in Kennington once more. A group of children were playing in the street with an old bicycle wheel rim that had been stripped of its tyre. A woman was on her hands and knees scrubbing her front step, while a couple of neighbours were passing the time of day on the other side of the road. As he looked up at the Queen's Buildings, it occurred to him how the brilliant blue sky was in marked contrast to the blackened buildings and deprived streets of impoverished London. His thoughts were broken as something knocked lightly against his ankle – it was the wheel rim the children had been wheeling between each other.

"Sorry, Mister!" said a small boy as he ran over to retrieve it.

The policeman smiled. "No problem, wee man, enjoy your game."

He left the children as they escaped into their own imaginary world, and prepared to continue with his own very real one. He referred to the three addresses given to him by Geddes: Charlie and Betty Williams at number 5, Mrs McAteer at number 17, and George Quinn at number 24.

Charlie Williams was the name that was sticking in Rab's mind. Assuming it was the same Charlie Williams who had been assaulted, his instinct kept pricking at him, suggesting the two crimes were somehow connected. He knocked at the door of number 5 but was immediately disappointed when there was no reply. After a couple of attempts, he moved on to number 17.

"Mrs McAteer?" he asked as an elderly woman opened the door.

"Yes?" She wore an expression of trepidation.

"There's nothing to worry about, Mrs McAteer. My name is Inspector Robert McKenzie of Scotland Yard." He showed her his warrant card, but this only served to worry the lady even more. "I assure you, you are not in any kind of trouble, Mrs McAteer, I would just like to ask you a few questions about a crime that was committed in the area recently."

"It's not them horrible Connors, is it?" she asked, gaining some composure after the policeman's reassurance.

"It is, as a matter of fact. Do you mind if I come in?"

Eileen McAteer opened her door and allowed the inspector through. "Horrible, horrible people," she said before McKenzie had even sat down, "they've terrorised everyone round here for years. Then when the war comes, all the young lads round here are going off to fight for King and country, while those two layabout sons of his somehow avoid being called up. It's a disgrace if you ask me. I don't know what the authorities are thinking about."

Rab smiled to himself: from being a timid, frightened old lady a moment ago, she was now a ranting mouthpiece, refusing to let him get a word in. When she paused for breath, he took his chance. "You've had dealings with the Connors then, Mrs McAteer?"

"Yes" – her head dropped with some embarrassment – "I lost my husband a few years ago, times have been hard. Since the start of war, things have got even worse. I had to borrow some money from them."

"When did you hear that they had been killed?"

She thought for a while. "It would be Monday . . . no, Tuesday. That's right, those young boys left on the Sunday, the money appeared on the Monday and word spread around that the Connors had been done in on the Tuesday."

McKenzie tried to unpick what was being said. "Which boys? What money?"

"All the local lads, the Kennington Pals. They left for France last Sunday. It was so sad to see them go. So handsome they were in their uniforms. God bless 'em, I wonder how many will come back."

"And you mentioned something about money?"

Eileen went over to the mantelpiece and picked up a brown envelope. "Yes, this appeared on Monday morning. There was a five-pound note in it. I didn't know where it had come from, it was just lying there on the mat. I asked Sissy next door and she said she had received the same, Dolly and Brian on the other side as well – they'd had ten pounds pushed through their letter box. It was the following day that we heard about the Connors and realised the money we had received on Monday was the same as what we all owed them."

McKenzie turned the envelope over as an instinctive act and saw the letters "WA" stamped in red on the opening flap. "Thank you, Mrs McAteer, that is extremely useful, I won't trouble you further. Do you mind if I take this envelope? I don't need the contents," he added with a smile of reassurance.

"No, you take it, love," she said, handing it across, "it's no use to me."

He left and went along to number 24. George Quinn was nodding over his newspaper when the knocking startled him. Opening his front door, he was surprised to see an imposing, well dressed figure.

"Mr Quinn? I am Inspector Robert McKenzie of Scotland Yard."

Albert Quinn's eyes widened as he gave a similar reaction to Eileen McAteer at the policeman's introduction.

"There's no need to worry, sir," said McKenzie, "you're not in any kind of trouble, I just want to ask a few questions about a serious crime that was committed in the area recently."

"The Connors," said Albert.

Rab smiled. "Yes, the Connors. Everyone seems to know about them."

"I knew the Connors and believe me they won't be missed around here, Inspector."

"Tell me, Mr Quinn, did you have any dealings with them?"

"I borrowed some money from them," said the proud man, ashamed of his involvement.

"And did you get that money back by any chance?"

"I did, as a matter of fact," said Albert, surprised at the policeman's knowledge. He disappeared from the hall for a few seconds and returned with an envelope; it was the same as the one Rab had taken from Eileen McAteer a few minutes earlier. "Inside was the exact amount I had borrowed from the Connors. From what I can gather, everyone else got theirs back, too."

The inspector looked at the rear flap of the envelope: it was stamped with the same red "WA". "Do you mind if I keep this envelope?" he asked.

"No, take it, it's no good to me," said Albert.

From where Rab was standing, on the doorstep of number 24, he could see across to the door of number 5, where he saw a man approaching and about to enter. "Thank you, Mr Quinn, that is very useful." He left the bemused tenant on his doorstep and hurried across as the man was opening his door.

"Mr Williams, is it?"

Charlie turned round.

Rab could see that the man's face was badly bruised. "Mr Charlie Williams?"

"Who are you?"

Rab took out his warrant card. "My name is Inspector Robert McKenzie of Scotland Yard. I am investigating three murders that took place last weekend."

Charlie didn't say anything – it was clear the policeman wasn't going to be put off.

"Can I come in?" asked McKenzie.

Charlie's wife, Betty, was coming through from the back yard with a pile of washing and gave a look of concern as her husband entered with a stranger.

"This is a policeman," Charlie said, and then turning, "this is my wife, Betty."

"Hello, my name is Inspector McKenzie."

Betty's face reddened and didn't say anything.

"Can I ask if you know a family called the Connors?" McKenzie was aware that everyone in the area knew the Connors but thought it was as good a place as any to start.

"Yes," replied Charlie, simply.

"Do you know that they were murdered a few days ago?" Again, he was asking a question he already knew the answer to.

"Yes, someone said as much."

"Tell me, Mr Williams, where did you get that bruising on your face?"

"I . . . had an accident at work."

"It's just that I have a report back at the Yard that tells me that a Mr Charlie Williams was beaten up and robbed after leaving The George pub a couple of weeks ago."

Charlie didn't reply.

"That was you, wasn't it, Mr Williams?"

Again, Charlie didn't say anything.

"Did the Connors have something to do with that?"

Again, nothing.

"Tell me, where were you on Friday and Saturday night last week?"

"I would have been either here or down at The George," replied Charlie at last.

"Do you have access to a gun, Mr Williams?"

"No."

"Did you receive an envelope through the letter box containing money on Monday morning?"

"Yes, we did," said Betty, "I don't know who delivered it."

"Was it for the amount you owed the Connors?"

"Yes," said Charlie.

"Do you still have the envelope?"

"I think it will be in the rubbish," said Betty, getting up and going through to the back.

"Is it just the two of you that live here?" McKenzie asked Charlie as his wife was searching.

"No, our daughter, Maureen, lives here. And our two boys usually stay here as well, but they've been called up. They left for France on Sunday." Betty proudly pointed to the picture on the shelf, showing her two sons in their uniforms.

"Part of the Kennington Pals?" asked the policeman.

"Yes, that's right."

"So they, and all of their colleagues, would have been here last week?"

"Yes. They arrived home from training on" – Charlie thought for a while – "it must have been around Wednesday, and they left for France on Sunday."

Betty returned with another brown envelope, identical to the others. Rab took it from her and looked at the rear flap. Something had been stamped on the flap like the others, but *unlike* the others, whatever it was, it had been covered with black ink.

"I may need to speak with you again, Mr and Mrs Williams, but in the meantime, thank you for your help."

Rab left the Queen's Buildings with plenty to ponder. The Connors had enemies throughout Kennington who had motive enough to see the back of their tormentors, but few had the means or the skills to carry out such a daring and vicious crime. The water was muddied still further by over a hundred local soldiers arriving that weekend who had access to weaponry and were now no longer in the country. The words "needle" and "haystack" were uppermost in the inspector's mind as he made his way back over the river.

# CHAPTER

# 9

# SECRETS

Much had happened in the few days between the Williams brothers' training and their deployment. Len was the last home on the night his brother had put paid to the Connors once and for all. Reg and Maureen had both gone to bed; both lay wide awake, however, and heard Len come in around midnight. It seemed that both brothers would be taking secrets with them to France the following day.

Everyone slept fitfully in the Williams household on the night of Saturday 5th August, each member alone with their thoughts, fears and hopes. The two lads were due to report to their barracks by ten o'clock the following morning, so – unwilling as they were, not to prolong the feeling of discomfort throughout the house – they quickly got up, washed, dressed, shaved and sat down for a quick breakfast with their parents and sister. They all sat in silence.

Privates Leonard and Reginald Williams then made their way to the barracks, knowing they would see their family at Waterloo station at four o'clock that afternoon as they left London for the last time. It was a rendezvous neither was looking forward to and when they arrived at the barracks, they found their Kennington Pal colleagues in the same subdued mood. It had all become very real.

They fell in at half past three that afternoon and marched off in double file towards the station. As they approached, the onlookers lining the streets thickened; by the time they arrived at Waterloo, the entrance and platform were packed with immediate family and friends.

Betty Williams burst into tears when the men were ordered to fall out and say their last goodbyes. She, in turn, started Maureen and Mary off. By the time Len and Reg found them among the throng, the three women were virtually inconsolable.

Len hugged Mary and said, "Try not to worry, love," trying and failing to sound convincing. "I'm sure it'll be fine and we'll be home before you know it."

Mary just sobbed into Len's shoulder. "I will pray every night for your safe return, my darling man and keep this close to you as a reminder of my love." Mary then gave Len the picture of her which Len had admired greatly,

"I will cherish it my darling it will never leave me," he replied as he put it in his tunic pocket.

Reg hugged his mother without saying anything. As they released their embrace, Betty reached for Len and the same agonising moment was repeated.

It was a scene being played out by more than a hundred families along the platform.

Reg hugged his sister and the two just looked at

one another, not saying anything, bonded by a secret neither could share.

A few hours earlier at noon, after the boys had left for their barracks, Maureen had made the excuse to her parents that she needed to speak with Mary and slipped away for an hour. But instead of visiting Mary, she went to the Woolwich Arsenal where she worked and, knowing that her colleague Jane Carter would be on her lunch break, she made her way to the stores. She knew exactly what she was looking for and exactly where they were kept. The stationery shelves were at the far end of a large store; she hurried along and slipped between two of the narrow, floor-to-ceiling racks holding the office equipment.

Her mother had asked why Maureen was going out with her big coat on, on such a lovely day; she had given the lame excuse that she thought she was catching a summer cold and didn't want it to get any worse. Betty was in no mood to question the odd reply on such a sombre day. The real reason Maureen was wearing her coat was that it had large inside pockets – pockets she was now proceeding to fill with brown envelopes. Once her pockets were full, she replaced the box from which she had taken them and slipped out, giving a curt I'm-not-in-the-mood-to-talk nod to anyone she encountered.

At the station, in the arms of her brother, she finally whispered, "I'll sort out the money tonight."

Reg nodded and hugged his sister with tears in

his eyes. "I'm sorry for getting you involved in this."

"FALL IN!" cried the platoon sergeant above the wailing and yelling.

The two boys gave their tearful sister and mother a final hug. Charlie Williams was too choked up to speak and simply shook the hands of his two sons, unsure as to whether he would ever see his boys again.

The Kennington Pals were transported by train from Waterloo to Southampton. Far from boisterous, the mood on board was quiet and sombre, each man lost in his own thoughts and worried about the family he was leaving behind. They then took the by-now familiar route of the British soldier, from Southampton across to Le Havre and then to one of the rest camps at Graville, five miles away.

Some of the lads took the opportunity of writing home: a few "arrived safelys" and a couple of "don't worries" were scribbled down, as much to reassure themselves as their loved ones. For his part, Reggie Williams just lay on his bunk in the darkness, staring up at the ceiling, wondering more about what he had left behind than what lay in front of him.

At breakfast the following morning, the Williams brothers and some of the Pals found themselves sitting with a few of their new London Regiment colleagues who had just returned from the front line for a few days rest and recuperation.

"What's it like?" asked one of the Pals, naively.

One of the regulars looked at him with a hard face and an empty stare. "Don't worry. You'll soon find out, son."

Another one added, "You'll see some kids playing in the villages on your way to the trenches. It's madness what's going on just a few miles further on."

"Hope you like bully beef," said another from further down the table.

Unable to make much sense of the rambling of their colleagues, the Pals fell in at nine o'clock and prepared to be transported to the Somme. They were told that they would be on a sixteen-day rotation: eight days on the front line, four days in the reserve trench, and finally, four days back at the rest camp.

"This rotation would then begin again and continue indefinitely!" screamed one of the many NCOs marshalling the troops in and out.

"If we're lucky," mumbled Reg Williams under his breath to his brother.

The first few miles of the journey east were taken by troop train; they then marched the last two miles towards the reserve trenches. On the way, they passed a battalion going the other way, presumably towards their four days of rest. Despite the fact that there were hundreds of soldiers on that dusty French road, not a word was spoken: the Pals marched forwards full of trepidation, while their colleagues marched the other way, staring vacantly ahead in what almost seemed a trance-like state. All the while, the sound of bombardment grew louder as the men advanced. When they finally reached their destination, they were greeted by another NCO from the London Regiment.

"WELCOME TO HELL!" he shouted. "We've been ordered straight up to the front line, so prepare to move up at one o'clock! Hygiene is important, men! When it rains, the trenches flood, so make sure you keep as clean and dry as you can, you don't want trench foot!"

"Lucky I brought that booklet Sergeant Lawrence gave us," mumbled Len, referring to their training in Catterick, which now seemed like a lifetime ago. "We would have been in real trouble, otherwise."

His mates were too nervous to laugh. They were given a lunch of bully beef and sweet tea, before falling in and moving up through the narrow dugouts that led to the front line. Up to this point, the young lads from Kennington – like the rest of the country – had only read about this place in the newspapers. It was so difficult to picture the actual scene from reading a few lines – almost as though it were a story being made up by an overenthusiastic writer.

But now, here it was, in stark reality. The front-line trenches were about six or seven feet deep, with wooden supports on either side and duckboards that had become as slippery as ice, due to the slimy mud that coated them, along the trench floor. There were dugouts where soldiers were slumped, trying to get some rest amid the cacophony of violence coming from the area above them known to all as no man's land.

"When we have to go into no man's land," shouted the sergeant who had led them forwards, you will not only encounter enemy fire, but you'll find yourself in an obstacle course of barbed wire and shell holes, all on a bed of mud."

"Fucking hell!" said Reg Williams to no one in particular. "What the hell have we come to?"

His mates agreed with the sentiment but kept their mouths shut, not that the sergeant could hear Private Williams anyway above the noise.

The Pals stooped and followed their sergeant along the line, passing men as young as they were, muddied and scratching at the lice and flies. At one point, they had to back against the wall of the trench as two stretcher bearers carried a soldier whose bare foot had swollen hideously to three times its normal size.

"That'll be coming off when he gets back to camp," said Len, referring to the man's foot, as the stretcher party passed.

"Lucky bastard," said Reg, "he'll be going home after that."

As he stepped back in line to carry on to wherever they were going, he nearly stood on two rats that were scurrying along the duckboards below them. Shaking his head in disbelief, Reg followed his brother in the khaki line that snaked along the muddy corridor. It was as though they were being put through a macabre initiation tour of the front line before they finally took up their position with another battalion – or what was left of it – from the London Regiment.

Like all new arrivals, the young lads from Kennington had to adjust quickly to this living hell. The Germans and their fortified – almost impenetrable – positions were one thing, the foul living conditions were another. On the first full day, Reg made a comment to his brother about the stench.

"A combination of the rotting corpses up top" – he gestured towards no man's land – "and those fucking latrines." He thumbed over his shoulder. "They're foul."

The first eight-day stint at the front for the Pals was unimaginable to anyone who hadn't experienced it themselves, yet strangely, despite the continuous shelling and explosions, and with the occasional sniper casualty, it didn't consist of any actual enemy engagement. The days began with "Stand-to" at five o'clock in the morning. If they had a chance, they had to try and attend to their personal hygiene, something made difficult by an army of flies homing in on each man as soon as he stripped. Trying to wash, shave and clean their teeth became a contest, a battle of wills that immediately dented the morale of many before the day had even started.

Once they had been split into platoons, their platoon sergeant would then lead them forwards to where they would take their place on the fire step, rifle in hand, just in case. Two hours would be spent sheltering from the shower of mud that rained down on them from the bombardment, unable to speak above the noise.

After two hours another platoon would come forward and give them a break from duty, allowing the first group to fall back and get some breakfast: fried, fatty bacon and hard biscuits, washed down with milkless tea. If washing was a contest, then breakfast was an unwinnable farce, as hundreds of flies covered the men's food and drink.

After their break, it was back to the fire step, where the noise by this time was almost deafening. The same routine as before for another four hours, until the platoon sergeant ordered them back for another break. It wasn't long before the Kennington Pals were participating in the gallows humour of the British Tommy: "What's on the menu today?" asked Sam Harris, the butcher's lad from Courtney Street, after the Pals had been at the front line for five days.

"Ooh, I think we've got the chef's special today," said Reg, "bully beef, with that extra layer of fat, black tea and that lovely plum and apple jam – the flies' favourite."

"Mmm," joined in Len, "I wonder what the army will then have in store for us this afternoon?"

"I'm sure we're due for a nice quiet one," replied his brother, "maybe a few board games or perhaps a gentle game of charades."

Reality was another four hours of bombardment, before the lads finally retired to the dugout to try and get some sleep, knowing that quality rest was virtually impossible – the flies would see to that.

Once the eight days were up, the Pals made their way to the reserve trench, where conditions were marginally better but no allowances were made as far as the food and the flies were concerned. Finally, they had the respite of knowing they were to enjoy four whole days back at the rest camp.

It seemed like an age since they had left Gravill. On the way back there, Len understood what the soldier had meant at the breakfast table when he said children were playing in the villages. He was right – Len experienced the strange sight of kids playing with a ball or a hoop, and people going about their normal business, while only a few miles away was the butchery and filth of the Western Front.

Once at Graville, the men's morale was lifted a little more when they found that packages had arrived from home. Letters and newspapers, socks and underwear. Len Williams volunteered to go and get some water to make a brew. "At last we've got something we can enjoy," he said as he left the billet.

The lads all got stuck in to opening their parcels as if they were children on Christmas morning.

"Cake!" cried Jack Winters as he opened his parcel, scoffing it down before he checked what else was inside.

"Here, look at this!" shouted Sam Harris as Len returned with a pan of water for the stove. Sam was reading a two week-old issue of the *South London Press*. "The Connors have been done in!"

"What do you mean?" asked Len as he lit the stove.

Sam read: "Three members of the same family were found murdered in their home on Kensington Road earlier this week. Jack Connor and his two sons, Robert and William, were known throughout the area and had long been suspected of illegal activities but had never been prosecuted. Speculation includes the involvement of another, rival, group in what one bystander termed a "turf war". Inspector Robert McKenzie of Scotland Yard is investigating the case but was not available for comment.

"Somebody finally done those bastards in!" concluded Sam.

"Yeah, they hounded my poor mum and dad for years," said Jack Winters.

The rest of the billet chorused their approval.

"That's a load off Dad's shoulders," said Len, looking at Reg, "at last a bit of good news."

No one had noticed Reg, who was just looking at the floor while his colleagues were toasting the demise of the villains.

"You all right, Reg?" asked Len, going over towards him. Reg didn't answer, or even look up. "Oi, Reggie," said Len, sitting beside him and shaking his shoulder.

Finally, Reg met his brother's eye. "Yeah, good news," he said quietly.

"What is it?" asked Len in a whisper while the rest of the billet was making merry. "I can see something's wrong."

"It's nothing."

"It's not nothing. Something's up."

Len took his brother by the arm and led him outside where they could talk more freely.

"Tell me what's going on." Reg didn't reply. "I know you, Reggie Williams, there's something you're not telling me." After a further delay, Len asked, "Do you know something about those Connors? Look at me!"

Reg lifted his eyes, knowing his brother would work it out anyway. "They had it coming, you know that, Lennie. We all know it."

"*YOU* D—" Len had to stop himself from shouting; he checked over his shoulder and lowered his voiced to a whispered hiss. "You did it? You killed them?"

"It was the night before we left. I told Mum and Dad I was going to The George but I went to see them instead. What they did to Dad was the last straw. I didn't think I had anything to lose with us coming over here; if I did them in, then the whole neighbourhood would be spared; and if they got to me first, they would be done for murder and put away. Either way, I would be doing the whole borough a favour."

"How did you do it?" asked Len, still struggling to come to terms with the revelation.

"I clubbed the old man with his iron" – Len suppressed a snort of laughter – "while this came in handy for the next one."

Reg took the push dagger from his tunic pocket.

"Where the hell did you get that?" exclaimed Len.

"Sergeant Lawrence gave it to me when we left Catterick."

Len shook his head and smiled at his brother; he could never resist his roguish ways. "Well, I suppose as long as we're over here, no one need know. The problem will come when and if we get back home. These people were animals but the law's the law, Reg, and no doubt Scotland Yard will be obliged to solve the crime.

"Still, let's worry about that another day. Let's go and have a cup of tea; I've still got my parcel to open." Len turned and then stopped. "Hang on, you never told me about the third one."

"Oh, I shot him," said Reg matter-of-factly. He pulled the Webley pistol from inside his tunic.

"Where the fucking hell did you get that from?"

"Oh, it was in the drawer of Connor's desk. Came in handy when Billy Connor showed up."

Len shook his head once more and put his arm round his brother's shoulder. "Come on , let's get that cup of tea."

They went inside to join their good-humoured colleagues, who were relieved to be spared the barbarity of the front line for a few glorious days. Len got a cup of tea and opened his parcel. Among the usual vital supplies was a letter from his beloved Mary. He read the letter and lay in silence on his bunk for the rest of the day.

# CHAPTER 10

# PROCESS OF ELIMINATION - 1916

The day after his questioning of the residents of the Queen's Buildings, Inspector Robert McKenzie sat in his office at Scotland Yard, looking at the three identical envelopes that lay on his desk. He turned them over and looked at the rear flaps.

"WA," he mumbled to himself, "WA."

He asked a constable outside his office to find Constable Geddes and his colleagues, who had helped the inspector with his enquiries to date. Ten minutes later, Geddes knocked on McKenzie's door and entered; behind him was Constable Donnelly.

"Morning, sir, you wanted to see us? I'm sorry but Beattie is out on patrol at the moment."

"Not to worry," said McKenzie, "you'll do. I want you to go back to the shops in Kennington" – he picked up the envelopes – "I want to know if anyone sells envelopes like these."

Geddes took the envelopes from the inspector. "No need, sir. My mum works at the Woolwich Arsenal factory and she gets her wages in an envelope like this every week."

"WA," said McKenzie, "Woolwich Arsenal, of course. In that case, go back to the Queen's Buildings and find out how many residents received envelopes like this earlier this week, and if they did, whether their envelope contained any money. Don't ask how much, just ask if they received one and if so, when they received it. Secondly, how many people in those tenements *work* at the Woolwich Arsenal. And if they do, I want to know where in the factory they work. Don't elaborate on the questioning – just, do they work there and where exactly do they work."

*Another laborious task,* each constable thought, but both knew that McKenzie was not a man to be argued with.

"Yes, sir, we'll get right on to it," said Geddes, escorting his colleague out of the office.

It was mid-afternoon when the two uniformed officers returned with the result of their questioning. Each carried a handful of envelopes identical to the three McKenzie was already in possession of. Geddes resumed his now regular role as spokesman: "Almost everyone in the tenements received these, sir," he said, holding a bundle in the air. "Here are the ones we collected and even the residents who couldn't provide theirs confirmed that they received the same envelope.

"We also found five individuals, sir, who work at the factory – one man and four women. The man is a fifty-six-year-old who started as an apprentice in the armoury and has been there ever since." Geddes flipped a page of his notepad. "A chap by the name of Carter . . . John Carter – he lives at number 12."

"And the women?" asked McKenzie.

"Yes, two of them work in the packing room" – again he checked his notebook – "Sarah Gallagher and Lucy Stride, and two of them work in the stores, Maureen Williams and Jane Carter, who is the daughter of this man John Carter at number 12."

"Williams – Maureen Williams?"

"Yes, sir, lives at number 5."

"The daughter of Charlie Williams." It was a statement rather than a question.

"Yes, that's right, sir."

McKenzie took the bundle of envelopes from the constables and quickly flicked through the reverse side, as though he was handling a large pack of playing cards. Each one bore the same "WA" stamp. And yet only one had had the stamp blacked out – the one received through the Williams letter box.

"That'll be all, lads, thank you."

Geddes and Donnelly raised their eyebrows at one another as they turned to leave; this was praise indeed coming from McKenzie.

The inspector segregated the blacked-out envelope. "Everything always leads back to Williams," he said to himself.

He thought for a while and decided that, rather than initially returning to the Williams household, he would visit the Woolwich Arsenal factory himself to see if he could find out anything further.

Thomas Male was nearing the end of his shift

when there was a knock on the store's door at the factory.

"A policeman to see you, Mr Male," said the young man who had been called to the gatehouse to escort the visitor through the vast factory.

Thomas looked up from his desk with some concern, wondering what he, or his staff, had done.

"There's no need to be alarmed," said the stranger. "My name is Inspector Robert McKenzie of Scotland Yard. You're not in any trouble, I just hope you will be able to help me with an investigation we are carrying out in the area."

Male nodded to the young man, signalling for him to leave, and gestured towards a seat by the desk he was sitting at. "Can I get you a cup of tea, Inspector?" he asked, suitably placated.

"No, thank you. I just want to ask you about the operation you run here in the stores."

Male looked at the vast warehouse of a store. "Well as you can see, we stock everything here from munition parts to stationery. As I'm sure you can imagine, at the moment we can't make stuff quickly enough – most of the hardware barely touches the shelves."

"Yes, it's actually the stationery that I want to ask you about," said McKenzie.

The storeman looked puzzled, after initially fearing that something had gone wrong with the munitions inventories.

"The stationery?"

"Yes," Rab pulled the envelopes from his pocket, "did these originate from the factory?"

Thomas only needed to glance at them. "Yes," he said, looking even more puzzled, "you can see the 'WA' stamp on the back. Where did you get them?"

The policeman ignored the question. "How many staff members work here in the stores?"

Male hesitated and thought for a moment. "Well, we try to have two people on each shift working round the clock, but sometimes that's reduced to one, as some of us have to go and assist elsewhere if the operation is short-handed. There are about eight of us, all told."

"Who was working last weekend?"

Thomas thought hard again. "Me and young Maureen Williams were working on Friday and Saturday, and young Jane Carter was on her own on Sunday."

"The two women you mention, would you describe them as honest and reliable?"

"Yes, good decent girls they are, from respectable homes."

"So, you have never had any cause to be concerned about them?"

"Never."

"When you were working with Maureen Williams, was there ever a time when she was on her own?"

"Not really, when I work with the two girls, I normally leave them on the desk here and I do all the running about fetching and carrying whatever is needed."

"And where are these envelopes stored?"

"Way down the bottom," replied Male, pointing, "with the rest of the stationery."

"So, Maureen couldn't have left her position here without being missing for several minutes?"

"No, I would have noticed her gone."

The policeman thought for a while. "Thank you, Mr Male, I think that is all I need for now."

"You're welcome," said Thomas Male, still uncertain as to exactly what had happened. "I'll get the boy to show you back out."

It was not the outcome Rab expected: if Maureen had been working on her own, she would have had ample opportunity to take the envelopes, but as she had been working with Thomas Male for the previous days, the suspicion now pointed towards this other young woman, Jane Carter.

McKenzie walked back to the now familiar tenements of Queen's Buildings and knocked on the door of number 12. A man of late middle-age opened the door; when the policeman introduced himself, the man confirmed that he was John Carter and that he worked in the armoury at the factory.

"Is your daughter in, Mr Carter?" asked McKenzie.

"My daughter? Why do you ask?"

"I would just like to speak with her about a matter in connection with the factory."

Carter was clearly uncomfortable with the situation but he reluctantly stood aside and allowed the policeman into his home. He took him through to the main living area where a young girl was sitting darning a shirt.

"Jane, this is a policeman, he wants to ask us some questions about the factory."

His daughter looked up with the same worried expression the other residents had adopted when McKenzie previously introduced himself.

"Thank you for your time, Miss Carter," he said, accepting John's gesture to sit. "I want to ask you about your work in the stores."

"Is something wrong?" Jane coloured.

The inspector took some of the envelopes he was carrying from his pocket. "Do you recognise these?"

"Yes," said Jane, clearly bemused by the question.

Rab turned to her father. "Did you receive one of these envelopes through your door on Monday or Tuesday of this week, Mr Carter?"

"No," replied John, equally bemused.

"You may be aware that members of a family called the Connors were recently murdered. May I ask if you have had any dealings with the Connor family?"

John Carter blew out his cheeks. "No I have

not! I've always made it my business to avoid those horrible people. We're good God-fearing people, Inspector McKenzie, but I can't say I will be losing any sleep over their passing."

The policeman turned back to Jane. "Are envelopes like these ever used for anything other than factory business, Miss Carter?"

"Not to my knowledge."

"Am I correct in saying you were working on your own on Sunday last?"

"Yes, that's right."

"Did anyone come into the stores and take a consignment of these envelopes?"

"No."

"And you didn't have cause to take them yourself?"

"No, why should I?" Jane was getting more confused by the policeman's questions.

Before McKenzie could ask anything further, Jane's father interrupted, "I thought you were working with young Maureen on Sunday?"

"No, I was on my own," replied Jane.

"Maureen Williams?" asked Rab.

"Yes, I saw her on her way out around lunchtime. She seemed in a bit of a hurry; I just assumed she had forgotten her sandwich and was rushing home to get it. The funny thing was, she was wearing her big coat on such a warm, sunny day."

"I never saw Maureen at all while I was working

on Sunday. I was on my own all day," repeated Jane.

"Thank you both," said the inspector, rising to leave, "you've both been very helpful."

Once again, his investigation was leading back to the door of the Williams household.

"My dad's not in", said the young woman who answered the door.

"It's not your dad I wish to speak to. Miss Maureen Williams, is it?"

Maureen was taken aback. "Yes."

"My name is Inspector Robert McKenzie. I spoke to your parents earlier in the week. Can I come in? I would like to clarify a few points."

"I told you, my dad is not in and I have company."

"And as I told *you*, it's not your dad I want to speak to. It's you. So, you can let me in or I can ask you to accompany me to Scotland Yard and I could question you there."

Maureen's mind raced with the events of the past week: Reg's crime, her collaboration, the possible consequences for them both. She stood aside and let the policeman in to where another young woman was seated in the living area.

"This is my friend Mary Eames," said Maureen, and then to Mary, "This is a policeman."

"Hello," said Rab before turning back to Maureen. "Miss Williams, you work in the stores at the Woolwich Arsenal?"

"Yes, that's right."

"What was your shift pattern last week?"

"I worked most of the week on the day shift with Mr Male."

"And on Sunday?"

"I wasn't working on Sunday."

"But you *were* at the factory?"

Maureen hesitated. "No, I wasn't."

"Miss Williams, you were seen around lunchtime at the factory."

"Oh, that's right," stammered Maureen, "I had to go in and give Jane a message."

"Jane Carter?"

"Yes, that's right."

"But you didn't see Jane, did you – or at least she didn't see you. I've just come from speaking with her and her father. It was him who saw you leaving the factory around midday." McKenzie didn't wait for Maureen to answer as he took the envelopes out of his pocket once more. "Do you recognise these, Miss Williams?"

Maureen didn't say anything. The policeman continued: "It is my belief that you took these envelopes from the store on Sunday. If you did, then it must have been you or an acquaintance of yours who filled them with amounts of money and delivered them to your neighbours here in the Queen's Buildings." He chose one envelope in particular. "This is the only one that had the 'WA' stamp scribbled out. It was the one that your mother discovered on the doormat on Monday morning."

Maureen looked straight at the policeman. "I don't know how those envelopes came to be delivered at Queen's Buildings."

"Where were you on Sunday night, Miss Williams?"

"I went to see Mary, briefly," she said.

"Yes, she did, she was with me, briefly," added Mary unconvincingly.

The experienced Inspector McKenzie was starting to admire Maureen's fortitude but he could spot a lie a mile away. "Ladies, I have dealt with many a criminal in my time and I know when someone is not being honest with me. Now, I do not believe that you are criminals, and I'm certainly not interested in some petty pilfering from the stores at the factory, but I am obliged to investigate three brutal murders that took place, probably on Saturday night last."

"Yes, I understand that, Inspector, but it's a pity that the police always seemed to turn a blind eye to some of the other criminals in our borough, don't you think?"

"I can't comment on how the borough has been policed previously, Miss Williams, but it is my job to investigate three brutal murders. That is what I am doing."

"You can't believe we committed the murders?" said Maureen, gaining in self-confidence.

"No, but I believe you may know who did. If

these envelopes originated from this house, then the money they contained did also. That money could have been taken from the victims' house, and therefore it is reasonable to assume that someone from the Williams household was present in the Connor household on the night of the killings."

"As I said, Inspector," said Maureen, "I have no idea how those envelopes came to be here."

McKenzie let a tense silence hang in the room.

"Where were all of the members of your family on Saturday night, Miss Williams?" he asked at last.

Maureen sat down slowly. "I was here with my mum and dad."

"I believe you have two brothers who left for France on Sunday?"

"Yes, Lennie went to see Mary," she said, indicating towards her friend.

"That *is* true," added Mary, virtually conceding that she had lied previously, "he came to ours and my mum cooked us dinner. He and I are sweethearts."

"And your other brother?"

"Reg . . . erm . . . I think he went down to The George."

"And if I went down to The George, would there be anyone there who could testify to that?"

"As I said, I *think* he went to The George but I couldn't be sure." Maureen knew that she had no other words that could make things any better.

Much to the two young women's amazement,

McKenzie cut the interview short and announced, "Well, that has been very useful, ladies, thank you. I will be back in touch if I need anything further."

He returned to Scotland Yard, satisfied that he had solved the case. He went straight to see Superintendent Lamb to report his findings.

"I think what happened, sir, was that one of these Williams boys went round to the Connors house that night and sought retribution for them beating up his father and generally terrorising the neighbourhood. He then took the money that the people in Queen's Buildings had paid and asked his sister to push it through their doors when he had gone. She, in turn, took the envelopes from the factory stores and did as he asked on Sunday night."

Lamb asked, "Do we have any hard evidence that proves the sister took the envelopes or was involved with distributing the money?"

"It's all circumstantial at this stage, sir. Unless someone actually witnessed her delivering the envelopes and came forward, it would be difficult to prove anything without a confession. What's more, this tight little community has been terrorised by these thugs for years – they're all so pleased to see the back of them, I don't think anyone would talk, even if they knew something."

"A right little Robin Hood, wasn't he?" said Lamb, referring to the perpetrator of the murders. "Taking from the rich and giving to the poor."

"There are no other suspects, sir. I think, on balance, this Reg Williams is our man."

"Unfortunately, Inspector, we have to play the part of the Sheriff of Nottingham. We can't allow brutal murders to take place and turn a blind eye. We need to make enquiries with the army and see where this lad Reg Williams is. If he is our man, we need to get him back here and hang him before the Germans kill him!"

# CHAPTER

# 11

# HALF TERM - 1970

The first challenge Tony faced during the half-term holiday was to tell his friend Mickey that he wouldn't be playing football with him in the park; he would not be meeting up with the rest of their mates; he wouldn't be wandering round the record shops in the Walworth Road or going to their favourite Wimpy on Saturday night. Instead, he would be spending most of the week in the library.

"The library!" exclaimed Mickey. "What are you doing in the library?"

Neither of them had actually visited the Kennington Library before. They had never been great studiers at the best of times and any books or learning materials they needed for anything, they always got from the *school* library.

Tony was a little embarrassed but told his friend anyway. "Well, I've been looking a bit further into that project we did."

"What project?" Mickey's piece on Crystal Palace burning down was a distant memory.

"You know, the one we did for old Smithy about local history."

"Well, that's what it is, isn't it – history?"

Tony didn't like losing face to his best mate, but the pull of the Williams boys' story was proving too great. "It'll just be for a couple of mornings," he said.

"Please yourself," said Mickey, more than a little put out, "I'll see you when I see you."

It was half past nine on the Monday morning of his school holiday when Tony found himself standing outside the ornate Victorian building. He was a little nervous; he couldn't believe there were many fifteen-year-olds visiting the grown-up building on their own, asking about back copies of newspapers.

He entered the large entrance hall with its high glass ceiling that filled it with daylight. An elderly man sat behind a large counter, his head buried in some reading material that lay before him.

"Excuse me, sir," said Tony, going over, "I wonder if the library holds any back issues of the *South London Press*?"

"Upstairs," said the man without looking up.

*A little rude,* thought Tony, but he gave him a "Thank you" anyway.

He went up to the first floor where he found the endless shelves of books overwhelming. *How could you find any book out of all these?* he thought to himself. At the far end of the floor was another large counter, identical to the one in the entrance hall. As he approached it, he saw a handful of people taking newspapers that were attached by a long rod to a stand; they found a seat and appeared to be settling in for the morning.

Not only was the counter identical to the one

downstairs, the man sitting behind it appeared to be the spitting image of his colleague: the same white receding hair, the same old baggy woollen cardigan and the same National Health glasses hanging precariously from the end of his nose.

"Excuse me, sir," said Tony politely, "I wonder if I could see some back copies of the *South London Press*?"

Unlike his colleague, at least this man looked up from his desk, although he made no attempt to disguise the contempt he held for the youngster. Usually, it was only serious historians who asked to see the back issues of the newspapers – now here was . . . a child!

"Why do you want to see them?" he asked.

*What, do you own them, mate?* thought Tony. "I'm doing a project for school, sir," he said instead.

"What project?"

"It's a project on the First World War – the Battle of the Somme."

"Which school do you go to?"

*What, are you going to check with old Smithy or something?*

"Beaufoy Comprehensive, just off the Lambeth Walk – do you know it?"

The man appeared to run out of stupid questions and reluctantly asked Tony to follow him. He took him to a large room on another part of the floor; the walls were lined with large ledgers containing newspapers from the mid-nineteenth century. The room had been full of murmurs and whispers until the librarian and the boy appeared; the six people in the room stopped and looked up from their studies.

"You will see the years marked on the shelves," said the man. He pointed to a four-step ladder that was on wheels, designed to access the higher shelves. "Use the ladder if something is out of reach. Take one ledger at a time and do not disturb the other people."

With that, the man left Tony to it. The eyes of the others never left him, as if offended by the presence of this stranger. *I've come this far,* he thought, *sod 'em.* He put down his bag at a vacant chair and scoured the shelves looking for 1916. The others finally conceded defeat and went back to their own work.

Tony started his studies in the issues of July of 1916, knowing that this was when the Somme offensive began. Details of the disaster of the first day appeared in the 10th July issue of the *South London Press.* Lists of the dead soldiers from the capital covered almost two pages. He stared at the staggering numbers of men lost, unable to visualise such a catastrophe. He ran his finger down the list; although there were nine men named Williams who had been lost, there was no mention of any Reginald Williams, nor any reference to the Kennington Pals.

His instinct told him that he was looking in the wrong place, so he continued turning the large sheets of paper, trying to be as quiet as he could be in the almost silent room. Among the constant war reports, he found a series of short paragraphs covering various local issues at the bottom of a front page from the last week in July. Among the paragraphs was one that reported a violent attack on Kennington Road:

And by the name of Charles (Charlie) Williams of Queen's Buildings was viciously attacked as he walked home last Friday night from The George pub. Mr Williams, a well-liked local character, works at Pegg's coal yard with his two sons, Leonard and Reginald. Robbery is believed to be the motive. Police investigations are ongoing.

*Len and Reg Williams!* thought Tony. *That has to be Mr Williams and his brother.* He scribbled down the details in the notebook he removed from his bag. He continued turning the pages of the various issues and finally found a reference to the Kennington Pals in the Monday 7th August issue. It was a story recounting the scene from the previous day, when the Pals had left for France. Tony was transfixed by a wonderful picture of the crowded platform at Waterloo station. There were hundreds of people in the photograph, seeing their young boys off. *Reg and Len must be among them somewhere,* he thought as he stared at the grainy picture, obviously taken from a high bridge above the platform. Tony sat wondering what could possibly have been going through the minds of the men who were leaving and their families who they were leaving behind. Unimaginable.

He continued going through the papers and in the 8th August issue found a headline that screamed "Vicious Murders in Kennington". Underneath was a picture of a body being loaded onto an ambulance on what Tony recognised as Kennington Road. He read the report of a family called the Connors who had been brutally murdered in their own home. It was suggested that they were a dangerous family themselves and the report speculated that the atrocity was probably the act of a rival gang.

So engrossed had Tony been throughout his studies that he had completely lost track of the time. He hadn't noticed that his fellow researchers had drifted away at various points of the day; he hadn't realised that he had gone without any lunch, and it was only now that he saw that the library would be closing in an hour. Deciding it was too late to get engrossed in more reading, he decided to return in the morning and pick up where he had left off, in the middle of August 1916. He put the ledger back on the shelf and made his way out.

As he was about to descend the stairs, the elderly man who had shown him to the research room in the first place appeared, coming up the stairs carrying a pile of returned books.

"Did you find what you were looking for, lad?" he asked, appearing to be in a more interested and helpful mood than during their earlier encounter.

"It was really interesting, thank you. I found some useful stuff but I am coming back tomorrow to see what else I can find."

"Was it information on the Battle of the Somme, did you say?"

"Yes, that's right."

"You want to go round to the Imperial War Museum and ask for Mr Graham. What he doesn't know about the First World War and the local regiments isn't worth knowing; but make sure if you are asking about any individual soldiers, you have their service number, regiment, rank and full name."

"Thanks very much," said Tony, surprised by the man's change in attitude, "I'll do that."

The following morning, he took the librarian's advice and instead of visiting the research room once more, he decided to call first at the museum to see if he could find this Mr Graham. He turned out to be a genial, welcoming chap whose enthusiasm for military and local history was apparent to anyone who met him. Tony explained what he was looking for.

"I believe Private Reginald Williams was part of the Kennington Pals, service number 4257," he continued. "I couldn't find his name in the lists of dead soldiers in July, but then found a piece in the newspaper that said they left in the August."

"Ah, yes, the Pals," said Mr Graham with a

reflective smile, almost as if he were there, "they went out and joined up with the London Regiment. I would guess that your man probably fell in the September fighting. Let's see what we can find out for you."

He led Tony up a flight of stairs and through a labyrinth of shelves and cupboards.

"Here we are," he said at last, "all the London lads' material is in here somewhere."

It was clear nothing was too much trouble for Mr Graham, as he was doing Tony's searching for him. Only a knowledgeable archivist could possibly hope to find any meaningful information among the sea of papers.

"Here we are!" he announced after about twenty minutes of searching. "Yes, as I thought, the regiment were part of the Fourth Army who fought in the Battle of Flers–Courcelette. Ah, here we go!" he said, discovering another file. "This is the war diary and the intelligence reports for the London Regiment. I'll bet our man was involved in this."

Tony waited patiently, amused by Mr Graham's nodding and continuous "aha"s; he was clearly as interested as Tony was in the findings. "Yes," he said, "the regiment were tasked with taking High Wood, a strategically important area that had been fought over since the battle began in July. There had been fierce fighting in the trenches around the wood for months; they finally took it in September with the aid of a tank battalion and a few Commonwealth battalions but suffered heavy losses in the engagement. There's actually a cemetery called The London Cemetery near the site."

"How many were killed?" asked Tony.

Mr Graham referred to the documents once more. "According to the War Diary and Intelligence Summary completed by H. H. Kemble Lt Colonel 1/24 Battalion London Regiment, casualties listed on 19th September were: 16 officers and 565 other ranks."

*Shit!* thought Tony, although he managed to avoid saying it out loud.

"That was just the London Regiment, remember," said Mr Graham, "it would only be a proportion of the total losses."

The two stood in silence for a moment, contemplating such slaughter.

"If I take you to the microfiche files, you will probably be able to find your man." Mr Graham showed Tony how to work the machine and gave him a large box of files. "They are in alphabetical order; no doubt there will be hundreds of Williamses but he'll be there. I'll leave you to it – come back and see me if you need anything else."

"Thanks, Mr Graham, that's great."

Tony sat for a further hour, first trying to fathom the workings of the machine and then going through the floppy sheets of film that contained the details of the soldiers who had died and whose names were Williams. Finally, he found 4257 Reginald Williams of the London Regiment, died 18th September 1916. That was it: he now knew when Mr Williams and his brother left for France, he knew what battle they took part in and he now knew when and where his brother Reg died."

"How are you getting on?" asked Mr Graham, who appeared once more.

"Very good, thank you, sir," said Tony as he switched off the machine. "I think I've found out most of what I wanted to. One last thing, I suppose – is it possible to find out where Private Williams is buried?"

"That would be easy to find out," said the curator.

He went to the large bookshelf adjacent to the microfiche files and reached for a ledger marked "British and Commonwealth War Graves Records". Turning the large pages of the book, he announced, "Here we go. Pte R Williams 4257 London Regiment died 18th September 1916. Here it is, sadly his body was not found. I do know, however, that his name will be found on the Thiepval Memorial in northern France."

He reached for another book on the same shelf. "The memorial reads: 'Here are the recorded names of the Officers and Men of the British Armies who fell on the Somme Battlefields July 1915 to February 1918 but to whom the fortune of war denied the known and honoured burial given to their comrades in death.' There is a reference: 9D 9C 13C 12. You will be able to see his name on the memorial using these references."

"That's very sad if that's all that's left," Tony said.

"Yes," Mr Graham agreed, "but there are over seventy-two thousand names of missing soldiers with no known resting place on the Thiepval Somme Memorial, so sadly, our man is not alone."

With his mission seemingly complete, Tony thanked the obliging Mr Graham once more and went home wondering whether it was appropriate to speak with Mr Williams again about his research.

He was still pondering this thought later in the week when his mum sent him round to his nan's with a few scones and biscuits she had baked for them.

"Aw, bless you, Tony!" said Nan when he appeared at her door with the surprise Tupperware box. "And that angel of a mum of yours. Come on in and I'll make us a cuppa – I'm sure she wouldn't mind us treating ourselves straight away."

She took him through to the living room where Mr Williams sat in his usual chair, in his usual dressing gown, with his usual ashtray close by.

"Hello, Mr Williams," he said politely.

"Hello, son."

Nan left them and went through to the kitchen. Tony was still unsure as to whether he should speak about his findings but he realised the two of them had nothing in common and therefore there was nothing else to speak *about.* After a few minutes of uncomfortable silence, Tony plucked up the courage to talk about some of the things he had discovered.

"Remember you helped me with my First World War project, Mr Williams? Well, I was down at the library and the War Museum the other day, looking at some of the information you were telling me about."

Mr Williams didn't say anything in reply. Unsure what else there was to talk about, Tony continued. "You must have been a real hero. I couldn't imagine what it must have been like over there."

Mr Williams stared at the wall opposite him. He then spoke for the only time when Tony would ever hear him on the subject. And yet it was as though he wasn't actually speaking with Tony; he was just staring at the wall, almost as though he was in a trance, transported back in time to over fifty years earlier and thinking aloud.

"We're standing on the fire step with five minutes to go. 'Fix bayonets,' came the command. Then it's zero hour and all hell breaks loose. There's our barrage, then there's the German's barrage and over the top we go. As soon as you get over the top, fear has left you and it's just pure terror. My good friend Sam Harris doesn't even make it out the trench. You don't look, you see, you don't hear; you listen. Your nose is filled with the smell of death. Civilisation has dropped away. It's barbaric. It's the nearest thing to hell on earth."

Tony's blood ran cold at what the old man said. He didn't know what to say in response and searched in his mind for something to take Mr Williams's mind away from such horrendous thoughts. Little did he know that he was about to aggravate the man's discomfort.

"Mr Williams, was your dad called Charlie?"

"Yes, he was," Mr Williams replied, returning his attention to Tony. "Why do you ask?"

"And did you and your brother work at Peggs coal yard?"

Mr Williams gave Tony a quizzical look. "Yes, we did, along with our dad."

"Well, when I was at the library the other day, looking at some old newspapers, I saw a report about a Charlie Williams being beaten up and robbed. I wondered if it was your poor dad, because it mentioned his two sons."

Mr Williams didn't say anything, so Tony continued. "It must have been really tough round here in those days." Still nothing. "There was even a report about some murders that took place on Kennington Road – some family called the Connors."

Mr Williams looked hard at Tony and the young lad suddenly felt uncomfortable. He felt that Mr Williams was going to speak, but something got caught in his throat, which led to a tickly cough, which, in turn, led to a full-on coughing fit.

Just then, Tony's nan appeared with a tray. "Oh, is he off again?" She put down the tray and went to pat him on the back.

"Maybe I should go, Nan," said Tony, feeling guilty that he had upset Mr Williams.

"You don't have to, love," said Nan as she carried on patting the old man's back.

"No, I think it would be best," said the young lad.

"OK, then, remember to thank your mum for the baking."

"I will, Nan. Bye, Mr Williams, hope you're feeling better soon."

He wandered home and after passing Nan's message on to his mum, went straight up to his room to look at the information he had found once more.

As he was leafing through the papers, something struck him for the first time. He referred to Len's handwriting on his army form. It reminded him of his friend Mickey's handwriting. Mickey was left-handed and wrote in an awkward – almost upside-down – style with his wrist forming a hooked shape as he did so. Tony used to tease him about it but found similarities in Len's handwriting on his army forms. He then compared the forms to the letters written to Mary and satisfied himself that they were written with the same hand. But he then realised that Mr Williams had written a note with his right hand

and given it to him when he ran an errand for him a few weeks earlier. He found the note in the pile of papers and compared the writing: it was completely different to the other writing of Len Williams. He then compared the note to the army forms of Reg Williams and saw that they were more of a match. *How odd,* he thought.

Tony was angry with himself for upsetting Mr Williams but at the same time, was intrigued by this latest discovery – another question he would like to ask the old man. He was also puzzled by Mr Williams's reaction to him referring to the newspaper reports about his father and the murdered family. Perhaps Mr Williams had known the Connors?

*More questions than answers,* he thought to himself. He wondered when he would get another opportunity to ask Mr Williams his latest questions, or even if it would be appropriate, given his reaction earlier. Unfortunately, the opportunity was destined never to arise: Mr Williams's health deteriorated still further over the next few weeks and a few days before Christmas 1970, he died, taking whatever secrets remained with him.

Thiepval Memorial Northern France
R Williams
9D 9C 13C 12

British and Commonwealth War Graves

British and Commonwealth War Graves

CHAPTER

12

# THE RELUCTANT GERMAN

The Kennington Pals had been on the Western Front for almost ten weeks. They were about to leave the rest camp for their third tour on the front line. The second had consisted mainly of digging more trenches, both at the front under heavy shelling and to the rear, to create more reserve and communication passageways. Each new trench was given its unofficial name: Regent Street, Piccadilly Circus, Old Kent Road. The officers' HQ was called Mayfair among other things. The trench to avoid was nicknamed Snipers Alley for obvious reasons.

Morale had been low and after three days of early-autumn rain, the act of digging seemed as futile as the whole bloody conflict itself. Reg Williams sank his blade into the ground for the umpteenth time; before he could wield his spade again, the narrow strip filled with water and disappeared. He looked at his brother – they were so close they had an almost telepathic understanding; both were thinking of their early training days at Catterick when Sergeant Lawrence had them doing this very task. "Character-building!" he would yell. They exchanged an ironic smile: there was no need to articulate their thoughts.

That had been a fortnight earlier; now they were housed in their billets being briefed on what was to come.

The Somme offensive had begun on 1st July, which proved to be the bloodiest day of the whole campaign: 60,000 Allied casualties, 20,000 of which had been killed. The Williams boys and their colleagues – along with the rest of the country – had read of the horror. Undeterred, the Allies persisted with the offensive for over ten weeks – without making any significant progress. The Kennington Pals witnessed first-hand that any new attempt to advance had repeatedly failed, and the whole initiative had ground to a bloody, muddy halt.

Now, it was their turn: a tiny number of soldiers joining the forty-nine battalions of the London Regiment, which, in turn, would replenish the thousands of losses in the Fourth Army, to see if they could unlock the stalemate.

It was late morning on Thursday 14th September; the men were packing their kits, gathering in their units and preparing to march to the front. It was a march they had already taken on two previous occasions, of course, but this time was different. They knew they were to be part of a further concentrated assault on German lines the following day. They had been briefed on the operation – something about the 56th Division's operations attempting to take an enemy trench near some funnily named wood. In truth, the lads took little notice of the strategic goals of the offensive; the numbers of troops involved were incomprehensible and they found themselves consumed by the thought of what had happened to the tens of thousands of their predecessors in the same area over the previous few months. They simply sat in silence, their minds wandering, wondering what fate had in store for them. The only thing that was drummed into them was that zero hour would be six-twenty in the morning, when they would be going over the top.

Lennie Williams took his brother to one side an hour before the Pals were due to fall in. "Reg, I've got something I want to talk to you about."

"You picked a fine time!"

"No, listen, this is important. You know as well as I do, there's a good chance that one or both of us won't make it back." Reg nodded. "One of the letters I got from Mary" – Len hesitated – "she told me she was pregnant."

"Fucking hell, Lennie!" Reg didn't know whether to congratulate his brother or commiserate with him. "You've got to get back."

Len shook his head. "There's no special treatment for anyone, Reggie, you know that. Listen, if I don't make it, there's something I want you to do. If you get out of this hellhole alive, you're gonna find yourself in more trouble when you get home. The police are going to be after you for the Connor murders; you know that for sure."

"I don't care about that."

"Well, you should! Think about it – surviving this insanity and then finding yourself on the end of a rope after doing your duty when others skived, and you did us all a favour by killing those bastards." Len looked over his shoulder and lowered his voice. "Listen, Reg, if anything happens to me, I want you to swap our identity tags."

"What!"

Len didn't let his brother speak. "I want you to swap our identity tags; that way, no one can touch you. If the police find out that Reggie Williams killed the Connors, and they will, then they'll also find out that Reggie Williams will be lying dead on the Somme."

"I can't do that, Lennie."

"You can and you will. Besides, I want you to do something else for me."

"What's that?"

"If I don't make it and you do, I want you to look after Mary and the baby for me."

Both lads – neither of them yet twenty – had tears in their eyes; Reg embraced his brother.

"Promise me," said Len.

"I promise," said Reg, swallowing hard, "but nothing is going to happen to us, we will both be having a pint in The George when this is all over."

The tender moment between the two brother was rudely disrupted by their Platoon Sergeant Bennett, who appeared in the doorway of the hut.

"WILLIAMS?...WILLIAMS BROTHERS?"

The two lads looked up when they heard their name called. Bennett picked them out of the crowd, "You two, Come with me!"

"Do we nee…" Lennie didn't finish his question as the sergeant disappeared.

The two looked at one another and left their pals, to catch Bennett up.

"What is it, Sarge?" asked Reg as they fell in alongside him.

"No idea! Follow me!"

The three soldiers entered yet another makeshift hut where a young lieutenant was studying a map that lay on a trestle table in front of him."

"Williams and Williams, sir!" announced Bennett when the three entered.

The officer looked up – he didn't look much older than Reg and Len.

"Ah, yes. You are from Kennington in South London, is that correct?"

"Yes, sir," said Len.

"You've been ordered to return to Le Havre and report to a Captain Richardson."

"What about, sir?"

"No idea, something about a local matter in Kennington. I've arranged for a vehicle to take you back. Dismissed."

With that, he went back to his studies while Bennett ordered the men outside where a troop carrier idled, waiting for its cargo. The brothers climbed in the back, their minds racing with what it could be about. Why a lorry just for us? and who is this Captain Richardson that he can take two soldiers from the front line no questions asked? and no unit mentioned; what is going on . The boys were used to being crammed in with another dozen or more men. They weren't focussing on the relative comfort, however.

"And get back here sharpish when you've finished or you'll both be on a charge!" shouted Bennet.

"Yes Sarge!" they both shouted back.

Bennett banged the side of the truck and the driver pulled off. After a few minutes Reg voiced what they were both thinking:

"It has to be about the Connors. They must have found out."

"It doesn't make sense though," said Len, "what are they going to do – send us home? They need as many men as they can get out here."

"What else could it be about then? He said it was something to do with Kennington?"

Len leaned back as the troop carrier bumped and bounced its way back to Le Havre, "I don't know, let's just wait and see, eh?"

Upon their arrival, a corporal met them and took them through the bustling camp and entered an unmarked prefabricated building at the far end. He ordered them to wait in an area outside an office until called.

One hour later "Come!" a voice called.

"Those Williams brothers are here from Kennington, sir," said the corporal as he opened the door.

"Show them in," said the voice.

The corporal turned to Len and Reg, "Captain Richardson can see you now."

He moved aside to allow the two to enter. The office walls were covered in maps while the captain made no attempt to hide a full ashtray of cigarette ends and a half empty bottle of Scotch and a glass that sat on his desk.

Richardson looked them up and down, "You are alike, aren't you?" he said. "You are the Williams brothers from Kennington?" how the bloody hell would he know what we looked like thought Len.

"Yes sir" he replied instead.

"I have an unusual task for you. In a few minutes time, a man will be brought in here in a blindfold. I do not want you to say anything, just listen to what he has to say."

Both brothers' foreheads creased in confusion as they looked at one another. Moments later, the corporal brought a man into the room dressed in a tattered German uniform. He was clearly a prisoner: dirty and his eyes covered with what looked like an old handkerchief that was secured round the back of his head. He also had his right arm in a sling, the end of which – cradling his hand – was caked in dried blood.

"Repeat what you said earlier," ordered Captain Richardson to the prisoner.

"My name is Johannes Kaufmann. Although I was conscripted to the German Army at the start of the war, I had only been in the country for six months."

To compound the brothers' confusion, the man clearly spoke with a South London accent. There was something vaguely familiar about him that neither could quite put their finger on. He continued:

"I am twenty years old. I was born in Frankfurt Germany. My father owned a Bakery on the corner of Newburn Street and Black Prince Road. My father's name is Willhelm Kaufmann but he was known locally as Bill Mann. I was known as John Mann The bakery was called Manns Bakery"

"Fuck Me!" exclaimed Reg. His brother grabbed his arm as a reminder of their orders not to say anything. Reg looked at Captain Richardson and mouthed the word "Sorry sir ."

The prisoner stopped his narrative at the interruption and turned his head in the general direction of where it came.

"Carry on," ordered Richardson.

Kauffmann continued, "I went to school with a lad called Reg Williams. He had a brother who was slightly older but the two were so alike, they were often taken for twins. We were good friends, played football together when we were kids and regularly went to watch Charlton Athletic play down at the Valley.

"The Kauffmann family had been bakers for generations in Frankfurt. I was born there but my dad wasn't happy there so he decided the family would move to London when I was two years old. London was all I knew until my grandfather died in Frankfurt in early 1914. My uncle asked my dad to return to Germany to help with the three shops the family owned. I didn't particularly want to go but my dad insisted as he said he would need a hand over there. As I say, we had only been there six months when war broke out and I was conscripted into the army. I hardly spoke German!

"When we were sent to France, because I spoke English, I was sent to the front line to act as an interpreter and see what I could hear from the British trenches. That's when I was captured during one of the raids and taken for a deserter."

There was silence in the room, before Richardson ordered his corporal to remove the prisoner.

"Well, what do you make of that?" he asked the two brothers, after the man had been led away.

Both Len and Reg were stunned. Their minds swirled with an element of relief that Reg's crime had not, after all, been discovered. And yet this meant that they would be going back to the front to re-join their comrades and whatever they were to face the following day. And now this, the revelation concerning their old friend John Mann.

"Yes, sir," said Reg at last, "That's John Mann all right. We grew up together. We would deliver coal to his dad's Bakery at least twice a week he was a regular customer. We always used to laugh to ourselves about his dad's accent. We thought he was Welsh."

"Welsh? Have you ever been to Wales?" asked Richardson.

"No, sir, I just thought…"

Richardson didn't see any point in continuing the inane questioning.

"They did move away from the area, sir," added Len. "We never really got to speak with John before he left. I suppose the family were in a bit of a hurry with his grandfather dying."

"So, you can vouch for this man? You think he is telling the truth?"

"Absolutely, sir. He was a good lad, I never thought we would come across him like this. I remember he even played the organ in the local church."

Reg added, "It's amazing that among the thousands of soldiers on each side, a bloke is captured who we went to school with and played football with. He even courted our sister Maureen for a couple of months if I recall."

"Yeah, that's right," confirmed Len, "I'd forgotten about that."

"All right," said Richardson, "I get the picture you've said enough. I can inform you two men that you've probably just saved this man's life. We believed he was a deserter or traitor given that he spoke English so naturally. He was captured during a raid by some of your London Regiment colleagues further along the line. He was about to be shot until he told us his story. It seemed far-fetched but then he mentioned you both by name and Pritchard out there" – he indicated to his corporal in the outer office – "said that the Kennington Pals were part of the London Regiment close by. In order to give the man a last chance, I sent word to your unit to ask if you could be traced. Luckily for him. It's a good job you were close by and both still alive".

Len and Reg stole a knowing glance at one another. Yes lucky for him and us they both thought.

"Would it be possible to speak with him, sir before we go back?" asked Len.

"I don't see why not. I believe your unit are due to leave for the front line in an hour. It's questionable whether you would get back in time for that anyway. A few minutes with your friend won't make much difference you can join up with your battalion later."

The captain called his corporal back in and ordered him to escort the Williams' brothers to see the prisoner. He was sitting in a medical tent with a few other wounded prisoners – they were not being attended to. When he saw his old friends walk in, his face lit up.

"Reg, Len – I don't believe it!"

"Hello John," said the lads moving towards him and then realising that they couldn't shake hands.

"We were just in the captain's office a few minutes ago when they brought you in," said Reg, "we couldn't believe it either!"

"I wondered what was going on," said John, "when they blindfolded me, I thought they were leading me out to the firing squad."

"Because you'd mentioned us and Kennington," said Len, "they tracked us down and brought us here to see if we could confirm your story. Luckily we could, so you're off the hook." He suddenly realised that his friend was being held as a prisoner of war and qualified his comment, "Well, at least you're not going to be shot."

All three shared a crooked smile, knowing that each of them was still in great danger.

"What happened to your arm?" asked Reg.

"A hand grenade was thrown into our trench. I tried to act quickly and throw it back out but just as I let go of it, it exploded. I lost part of my hand as well as damaging my arm and the side of my neck."

He tilted his head to the side to reveal sickening burn marks under the hair line of his head.

John lifted his arm "And no more organ playing for me," said John, "another thing this bloody war has taken.

"What will happen now?"

"I'll probably get shipped back home – to England that is – to a POW camp. How strange is that?" In an effort to change the subject, he asked, "How's your dad then lads – still playing dominos down the George?"

"Yes, he's doing all right," said Reg, quickly, not wishing to dwell on the condition of his dad, or the problems he left him and his sister with."

How about you and Mary Eames Len, have you proposed yet? "Not yet but as soon as I get back I will." replied Len.

"And dare I ask about Maureen?" It was clear John was still sweet on the lads' sister.

"Yes, she's doing well," said Len, "she works at the Woolwich Arsenal factory these days."

"Plenty of work for her then," said John with another smile. Then a thought came into John's mind "I wonder if I could ask a favour?" He fumbled awkwardly in his tunic pocket with his left hand and pulled out a ring. "This isn't anything significant but I wonder if you would give this to Maureen for me when you get back and just ask her if she would keep it safe for me until this is all over then I'll come and collect it in person. I don't think she thought much of me but, I thought an awful lot of her. If we hadn't moved away, I'd like to think things could have been different between us and I could have worn her down into liking me."

"I'm not so sure about that." said Len

The three friends shared a chuckle.

"Williams!" Corporal Pritchard appeared at the tent flap, "it's time to go move yourselves"

Reg took the ring from John, "I'll make sure she gets it, mate."

The three looked at each other, almost certain that they would never see each other again. Their discomfort was ended by a "Come on!" by Pritchard. Len and Reg said their goodbyes and left their friend to his fate.

CHAPTER

# 13

# FIX BEYONETS

*"ALL RIGHT MEN, FALL IN!"*

As the Williams brothers were talking to their old friend, five miles away their battalion colleagues were being yelled at by a dozen or more platoon sergeants.

It was time for them to move up to the front.

As the Kennington Pals were falling in, a corporal from the Signals Office picked his way through the crowd of soldiers and approached one of the platoon sergeants.

"Do you have a Private Williams, Sarge?"

"How the hell do I know," replied Sergeant Deakin – a tall no-nonsense character, focused solely on moving his men to the front. "I've just been assigned to this lot, I don't know who any of them are!"

"It's just, there's been a telegram come through from HQ for a Private Williams. The police want to speak with him apparently."

"The Military Police?"

"No, Scotland Yard."

"*Scotland Yard!* They can bugger off! Unless they can stop the war while they look for their man of course. No? I thought not. Give me the bloody telegram and if I come across him, I'll let him know."

The Kennington Pals set off for the front as part of the first battalion of the London Regiment. As they were doing so, Len and Reg Williams were an hour behind them, making their way back to the camp from Le Havre. Once there, it had been arranged that they would follow their colleagues as part of the second battalion, made up of Pals from Kent County, Lewisham and Islington. At the front, they would then be directed to join their own battalion.

"Fancy meeting John again amongst all of this insanity," said Reg to his brother, as the truck made its way back along the muddy road, "I thought I was done for, when we were called out."

"I bet John did as well," replied Len without intending to sound facetious. As if to remind them both of what they were going towards, he added, "Besides, I don't know what would be worse, taking your chance at the Old Bailey or facing Fritz over here."

The two barely had time to retrieve their back packs and rifles before they were ordered to fall in and move up to the front.

It had been raining for days but the soldiers were oblivious to the weather, as they loaded onto the troop carrier in silence, alone with their thoughts. Once they disembarked to march the final couple of miles to the trenches, more than one had to leave the line momentarily to vomit into the ditch by the muddy road. Len and Reg were instructed to pick their way through a crowded trench to the allotted position of the Kennington Pals, a few hundred yards further on. Hundreds of men now crammed into the narrow channels. Amid the cursing and shouting, soldiers jostled each other as they moved back and forth to assume their station, all the while under heavy shelling from the enemy position›s

Once they found their battalion, the stark reality of what they were facing became apparent. Twenty minutes earlier, their trench had taken a direct hit from a heavy mortar shell. Sam Harris sat on the fire step spattered in blood and body tissue.

"*SAM!*" cried Len, when they saw him, "are you hurt?"

The young lad was in shock as to what he had seen.

"No, he's all right," said Jack Winters from behind them, "he was just beside Sergeant Bennett when he took the full force of the blast. He's covered in what's left of Bennett. Four others got it as well – Bird, Campbell, Black and young Carr. At least it was over quickly for them."

Len and Reg looked at each other in disbelief: *what the hell were they doing here? What was it all for?*

A different voice sounded and interrupted their thoughts, "You men give these lads a hand to clean up the mess."

Len turned to see a new man with a corporal stripe barking out orders, presumably after receiving a very quick field promotion following Sergeant Bennett's death. He decided it didn't matter who was ordering who to do what – orders were bloody orders and they had no choice but to participate in this continuous carnage.

In a state of abject disbelief, they spent the following two hours clearing away the various body parts of their friends and colleagues. As dusk fell, Len, Reg and the others who witnessed the blast but were lucky enough to avoid injury, returned – filthy, exhausted and traumatised – to their fox holes where they found a brew waiting for them. As the ground vibrated with the ever-present rumble of distant explosions, the men sat in silence, caked in mud and the dried blood of their friends, trying to make sense of the day's events.

After what seemed like an eternity, it was Reg who spoke quietly to his brother.

"I've just realised, earlier today we were called away to see John Mann. Captain Richardson told us that we probably saved John's life. The irony is that he also saved ours. If we hadn't been called away, we would have been here on this very spot. We'd probably be dead now.

One of the NCOs who was sitting close by overheard Reg's whisper, "You're right, son," he said, "you don't have to be a good soldier in this war to stay alive, you just have to be a lucky one."

As dusk turned to night, the men were ordered

into their line; one line of dozens. Allied troops from across the Empire all dutifully in position waiting for the following morning. They found themselves so tightly packed, there was no room to lie down for what was going to be an extremely uncomfortable night; leaning against the side of the trench while trying to keep their footing on the muddy duckboards became almost ridiculous. Each had a rifle and bayonet, and a heavy backpack, from which hung a gas mask. Most men leaned against the side of the trench and each other to try and doze the night away. One of the few sounds that could be heard was that of some of the young lads sobbing with fear and others just mumbling to themselves.

Midnight passed the waiting was excruciating. By four o'clock the first slivers of light had appeared over the battlefield and the men prepared to go. Not long now. At six, tanks that were due to follow the infantry rattled into position while artillery from both sides commenced.

"Fix bayonets" came the command. At quarter past six privates Leonard and Reginald Williams, along with the other young lads from Kennington, climbed up onto a fire step in a trench on the Western Front, north of the River Somme. The seconds ticked towards zero hour; hearts thudded, stomachs churned; some men were heard crying, some were just mumbling to themselves, but most stood in numb disbelief as to what was about to happen.

With thirty seconds to go, a terrifying silence fell over the battlefield as thousands of men froze in the unbearable anticipation. Scores of commanders stood with whistles in dry mouths watching the second hand move around the dial for the final time.

"Stick close to me Reg!" shouted Len. "I'm right behind you Len," came the reply. Finally, at six-twenty high-pitched whistles relayed along the trenches to signal the start of the attack – it was time to "go over the top". Thousands of British soldiers tried to clamber up the slippery ladders, scramble out of the trenches, pick their way through their own barbed wire and then spread out into the straight line in accordance with the plan, before walking forwards and getting what shelter they could.

The whistles of the British commanders not only acted as a signal to their own men but also alerted the German machine gunners as to what was about to happen, and as the British troops appeared above ground, the slaughter began. Such was the intensity of the machine-gun fire, some men never made it to the top of the ladders – Len Williams gasped in horror as he saw Sam Harris getting hit and his body gently slide down the sloped parapet and back into the trench. The noise was incessant; both the Williams lads made it out of the trench but within ten yards, Reg found his heavy pack snagged in the barbed wire that had been originally constructed to protect the Allied trenches. Now, it was little more than a deathtrap. He managed to struggle his way out of his backpack and wrenched himself clear of the barbed wire, losing his footing in the process; machine-gun fire whizzed past his head and found a target in the man behind him. Reg glanced back to see twenty or more soldiers rendered helpless in the barbed wire – unable to avoid the murderous machine-gun fire, their dead, bullet-shredded bodies hung suspended in the mesh alongside his now ownerless backpack.

Len reached down and helped his brother to his feet. Platoon sergeants were shouting orders to their men that couldn't possibly be heard above the din of the machine-gun fire and the death screams. As his battalion advanced across no man's land, it was impossible to distinguish who or where his Kennington Pal colleagues were in the bullet- and shell-swept open ground. He was just aware that, amid the mayhem, khaki uniforms were falling left and right, cut to pieces by the indiscriminate fire from the opposing trenches. Within minutes, the whole area was littered with limbs and bodies.

Reg had made about fifty yards and spotted one of the machine-gun nests through the smoke and chaos. He saw a mound in front of him and dropped flat to take aim; it was only when he was prone that he realised he wasn't leaning on a mound of earth but on a dead horse that had obviously been lying there, decomposing, for days if not weeks. Its flesh had rotted away exposing its ribs, while its staring eyes appeared as shocked and frightened as that of any human thrust into the same unimaginable horror. Reg lay and took aim anyway, firing several rounds into the nest; whether he hit anyone or not he couldn't be sure but at least he was doing something in all this futility.

"REG! REGGIE!"

Reg turned at the sound of his name and saw his brother to his right; he and a few others had found a little shelter in one of the hundreds of craters left by the shells and mine explosions. Reg scrambled across on his belly and slid down the muddy wall of the crater to join his brother and around half a dozen others who had found valuable cover. No sooner had he regained his footing than another shell exploded just above them, knocking him and the others off their feet. The headless body of a British soldier was catapulted into the shell hole as a result, while one of the lads in the crater – neither Len nor Reg knew him – screamed in agony as he realised his leg had been blown off at the thigh. Blood gushed from the stump and trickled into the large muddy puddle at the base of the shell hole. The young man gradually went quiet, as if somehow relieved that certain death was now only minutes away.

"YOU STILL WITH ME?" shouted Len to his brother.

Reg gestured with a nod. He looked beyond his

brother and saw that one of the men was an officer – he didn't recognise him – from his own regiment.

After a few deep breaths, the officer shouted, "RIGHT MEN, PREPARE TO PUSH AGAIN! ON MY MARK!"

He counted three on his fingers and then signalled the advance. The men who were left clambered up the side of the shell hole and back out onto the main hellscape.

No sooner had they appeared above ground than Reg slipped and fell once more on the treacherous surface – by doing so, he inadvertently avoided the blizzard of machine-gun fire his brother and the others ran into. He dropped his rifle and let out a guttural scream as he swivelled on the ground: "LENNIE!" He watched – as if in slow motion – as his brother and colleagues were driven back into the shell hole through the sheer impact of the machine-gun bullets.

Reg scrambled back into the crater as his brother was uncontrolledly sliding down the muddy wall into the puddle of filmy blood-stained water on the base. He came to rest against a limbless corpse that – judging by its condition – had lain there since a previous assault. Reg rushed to attend to his brother and took him in his arms; he saw he was riddled with bullets.

"LENNIE! LENNIE! FUCKING HELL, LENNIE!"

Len was drifting in and out of consciousness – they both knew there was no hope. Reg could not contain himself as he wailed over his mortally wounded brother, tears mixed with mucus that streamed from his nose and mouth onto Len's bloody tunic. It was as if the chaos created by the thousands of men around them didn't exist – Lennie and Reggie Williams were alone with each other.

Len became momentarily lucid and opened his mouth, indicating his brother should lean closer. "Reg," he murmured, "remember what I said. Take my tags."

Reg somehow summoned the ability to speak through his choked throat. "But Lennie—"

His brother interrupted him. "Take my tags, Reggie, and put your tags on me, it's the only way . . . Look after Mary and the baby for me, please, Reggie, you promised. There is a letter in my pocket for Mary . . . please take it" – Len's breathing was getting more erratic as he gasped his words out – "when she reads it she will understand and tell her I love her so very much. Get yourself out of here and tell . . . tell Mum, Dad and Maureen that I love them."

The effort summoned up to speak took what little energy Len had left. He died in his brother's arms.

"NO!"

Weeping uncontrollably, eighteen-year-old Reg Williams slipped his brother's identity tags from around his neck and put his own around Len's. He put on Len's tags, took the letter addressed to Mary from Len's tunic pocket and put it in his own. Whilst taking the letter the picture of Mary fell out. Reg looked at the picture and then carefully placed it back in Len's tunic breast pocket close to his heart. Finally, he kissed his brother on the forehead and resolved to carry out his wishes. "I promise," he whispered.

He suddenly became aware that the noise coming from behind had subsided, yet there was cheering – getting ever louder – coming from the advanced positions. The Germans had left their trenches and were seeking to press home their advantage!

No sooner had Reg realised this than four, then five German soldiers appeared at the mouth of the shell hole in which he was lying among a dozen or more bodies. The scene beheld by the German soldiers caused some hesitation among them, as it looked as though all the Tommies in the crater were dead. Despite his blood boiling with fury, the hesitation allowed Reg a few valuable seconds to clear his head; he had lost his rifle but reached into his sodden tunic and pulled out his stolen Webley pistol. He fired off four rounds in quick succession and two of the Germans fell; two others lost their footing, such was their surprise at being shot at from a pile of dead bodies, and slid into the shell hole, dragging the last of their colleagues with them. Reg off-loaded the final two rounds into one, killing him instantly, while another wrestled with his rifle in an effort to regain some balance and composure. He was too late: Reg picked up a discarded rifle and crashed the butt into the man's forehead with such force he felt the man's skull shatter under the blow. The man's eyes rolled back in his head and it was clear he was dead before his body splashed into the mud. The final German had regained his footing as his colleague fell, and turned to rush at Reg but the young lad was too quick; he withdrew the push dagger from his tunic pocket and thrust it into the neck of his enemy. Unlike the previous occasion when he had used the weapon, Reg punched the dagger into his victim over and over again, venting his fury at the loss of his brother. Reg felt the warm blood of the soldier run down his hand until it reached the sleeve of his tunic.

His anger still not satisfied, Reg decided to clamber up the side of the shell hole with a view to attacking any German survivors with the murderous blade. As he was scaling the muddy ascent, however, he heard the dreaded cries of "GAS! GAS! GAS!" relaying along no man's land. Sure enough, he looked up to see a malevolent cloud creeping over the top of the crater. Having already lost his gas mask and supplies in the barbed wire earlier, Reg darted his eyes around the bodies strewn about him to see if any still had their mask attached. Incredibly, the one gas mask was attached to his fallen brother's pack. He checked once more that his brother was dead – he would have given anything to swap places instead of identities – before taking his mask and putting it on.

As he was about to scramble out of the shell hole and attempt a return to the Allied lines, he heard a sound from one of the bodies.

"Help! Help!"

He turned to see that the officer who had led them over the top of the crater was badly wounded but still alive. Reg went to tend to him and saw that he didn't have a mask either. As the gas started to fill the crater, Reg took three deep breaths and put the mask on the officer; he then put his shoulder under the man's armpit and dragged the limp body back out onto what a few minutes earlier had been a deafening killing field, but was now a silent plain, shrouded in a deadly mist. Any wounded who lay in no man's land were destined to suffer a further agony.

Reg kept alternating use of the mask with the officer while trying to haul his body back to the trenches. Once he was in sight, two stretcher bearers from the Royal Army Medical Corps saw the two struggling towards them and made their way out to assist with an extra mask.

Coughing and retching, Private Williams and the officer were lowered back into the Allied trench before the two medics took them to a dugout that was being used as a first-aid post.

Drowsy from the gas, with both eyes stinging, and exhausted from his exertion and traumatised by the loss of his brother, Reg waited among the horrendous mass of congestion and suffering. The scene resembled more of a butcher's shop than a first-aid post. Casualties were everywhere. After an initial assessment, they were being evacuated to the nearest static medical operational units behind the lines, known as field ambulances. Finally, when their turn came, Reg and the officer – Reg still didn't know his name – were assessed and given some water.

"Private Leonard Williams – London Regiment!" he heard the medic who was attending to him shout to an orderly. The man had referred to the identity tags around Reg's neck.

It was only then that the full comprehension of what had happened dawned on the younger brother. He broke down and wept.

"Trauma and gas inhalation!" cried the man. "Captain James Palmer – London Regiment!" the man then shouted, referring to the officer he had rescued. "Bullet wounds and gas inhalation! Get both these men to a Clearing Station.

The Casualty Clearing Stations were further back out of range of the enemy artillery; Private Williams and Captain Palmer joined hundreds of other men being moved to No. 23 General Hospital, ten miles behind the front line. Once there, they were both diagnosed as having “Blighty wounds”: wounds from which they would survive, but which were serious enough to prevent them from resuming active service.

After less than three months in France, Reg was going home. But his escape came at the heaviest cost; his brother was one of tens of thousands of soldiers destined to be left dead on a foreign field, never to return. And yet as far as the rest of the world was concerned, Leonard Williams *was* returning to England.

CHAPTER

# 14

# GOING HOME

Reg Williams lay in his hospital bed in Rouen in northern France in a state of shock. The things he had seen could not go unseen; they were images that were imprinted on his brain and he knew they would live with him for the rest of his life. And worst of all, he was haunted by the memory of losing his brother and leaving him lying in that waterlogged shell hole to rot away like so many before him .

Lying in the bed opposite Reg was Captain James Palmer, the young officer Reg had saved during their retreat from the gas attack. Like the Williams brothers and their Kennington Pals, Captain Palmer was on his first deployment to the Western Front. The son of a West Country solicitor, he had received a temporary commission under the new system that had been introduced for training officers following his service through the Officer Cadet Training Unit. Despite his having no affiliation with London, in the needs-must environment of the Great War, Palmer had been allocated a commission with the London Regiment. In the chaotic disorder of no man's land, he had found himself in a muddy crater with a group of soldiers that included Reg and Len Williams.

Military rank and societal status counted for

nothing in the hospital ward: an officer from a middle-class family in Trowbridge and a coal yard worker from a working-class family in South London lay with the same vacant stare in their eyes, along with the dozen or so other men in their ward and the hundreds of others throughout the hospital. Some moaned in physical pain; others coughed following the gas inhalation; no one spoke.

Such was the traumatised state of the soldiers that two orderlies were going round each bed, one referring to each man's identity tags and comparing the details with those that the other had on a clipboard.

"Captain James Palmer, London Regiment said the first. "Yes," replied the other, having referred to the numerous sheets on his board before ticking the appropriate box. "Private Michael Jones, Canadian Corps . . . " "Yes." "Private George MacLean, Northumbrian Division . . . " "Yes." And so it went on, up and down the ward, logging Allied soldiers from New Zealand to Scotland. "Sergeant Charles Deakin, London Regiment . . . " said the first orderly at the penultimate bed in the ward. "Yes," replied his colleague. And finally, "Private Leonard Williams, London Regiment . . . " "Yes."

At the sound of his brother's name, Reg snapped out of his mental agony, only to immediately comprehend that his brother had not made some miraculous recovery and escape. Instead, he had the stark realisation that this was the first day of the rest of his life under an assumed identity.

"Williams?" said the man in the next bed. Sergeant Charlie Deakin looked over at Reg. "Of the London Regiment?"

"Yes," replied Reg.

Although, like Reg, Deakin had been a member of the London Regiment, such were the numbers of men involved and the chaos of assigning NCOs to platoons, the two didn't know each other. They may have been in reasonably close proximity on the fire step, any formation had been lost once they went over the top. Like the Williams brothers and all the other Allied troops, Deakin became embroiled in the every man for himself madness of no man's land. He had seen his own leg crushed in an explosion and somehow made his way back to the British lines, only to receive an emergency amputation. The previous days had been a blur and yet the sound of hearing the name "Williams" triggered a recollection of what was probably the least memorable incident of the previous seventy-two hours.

"I've just remembered I had a telegram for a man named Williams given to me before we left the rest camp."

Reg didn't respond.

Deakin searched through the nightmarish images of his memory for a recollection that probably meant very little now. He looked around to see if his tunic had survived his evacuation from the front – it had not.

"That's right," he said after a while, "it was something about Scotland Yard wanting to speak with him."

Reg went cold at the thought; without ever having received any telegram, he knew exactly what it was and the purpose of it. He wondered about Maureen's safety: had she been arrested? What would happen to her if she had? He glanced across at the chair beside his bed, upon which sat what few belongings had been brought with him. Unlike Sergeant Deakin, Reg's tunic was there and he reached across. The mud had dried on the khaki, making it like stiff cardboard to the touch. He searched the breast pockets and retrieved the letter given to him by his dying brother, addressed to Len's sweetheart Mary. The dirty envelope was wrinkled after being stained in the bloodied, muddy water and then drying out. Reg slipped the envelope under the sheets of his bed, silently vowing to always keep it with him until he returned to London.

"Well, the only reason the authorities would want to speak with this particular Williams," said another voice, "would be to give him a bloody medal for bravery."

Captain James Palmer had heard Sergeant Deakin's reference from across the ward. "The chap saved my life and I shall be eternally indebted to him." He then addressed his saviour directly: "When I am fit enough to file my report, Williams, I will recommend that you are at least mentioned in despatches for your bravery. As I was lying there helpless, I witnessed you kill those German soldiers that came pouring into our shell hole."

"Thank you, sir," said Reg, "but I'm no different from anyone else. I think we all deserve a bloody medal for bravery, but sadly there are too many who won't receive anything." Reg then started to cough uncontrollably; an orderly rushed to wipe the blood that streamed down his face. *Mustard gas kills eventually,* thought the orderly.

Reg's family were about to receive the worst possible news. At ten o'clock on the morning of Sunday 1st October 1916, there was a knock on the door of 5 Queen's Buildings. Charlie and Betty Williams instinctively looked at one another, sensing something was horribly wrong; they weren't expecting anyone. Charlie went to answer the door, while his wife followed slowly behind him.

Opening the door, Charlie's worst fears were realised: before him stood the terrifying sight of a young telegram boy, who held out a small brown envelope. The young lad – now a veteran of his dreadful duty – didn't say anything.

Before he even took the telegram, Charlie looked over his shoulder at his wife Betty who had appeared in the hallway, instinctively fearing the worst. Charlie mustered up the courage to take the brown envelope from the boy and opened it.

"It's Reg," he said simply.

Betty collapsed to her knees and screamed her agony.

Maureen came running through from the yard where she had been rinsing her clothes in the wash house. "What is i . . . ?" She stopped when she saw her mother on her knees wailing uncontrollably; her eyes moved to her father, who still stood at the front door with a telegram in his hand and a vacant expression on his face. Maureen sank to her knees and joined her mother in her unimaginable agony.

The next day or two saw a procession of well-meaning yet intrusive visitors, offering their If-there's-anything-I-can-do's. Betty was numb to it all; Charlie was annoyed by it; Maureen was weighed down by guilt. All of them just wanted it to stop. But it would never stop: a further note arrived from the War Office a few days later. Charlie saw it was different from the last but dreaded opening it all the same.

"Len's coming home," he muttered.

"What?" said Maureen.

Charlie looked up. "It's Len, he's coming home. Apparently, he's been wounded. He's in a hospital in France and can't go back to the front so he's being shipped home."

No one said anything. The three just stood in silence, their emotions swirling as they tried to take in this latest news. What did it mean? How badly was he injured? Would they send him back once he was better? Would he ever *get* better?

"I'll go and tell Mary," said Maureen at last.

When she did so, Len's sweetheart was overcome, swamped by feelings of relief that her love was still alive combined with concern as to his condition and guilt knowing that his brother Reg was dead and the family were still coming to terms with their loss. She burst into tears and the two friends fell into each other's arms.

It was Monday of the following week that the latest number of wounded soldiers from the London Regiment were due to arrive, following what would no doubt be an uncomfortable midnight crossing from Le Havre. Whereas two years earlier, hundreds of troop carriers had crossed the Channel taking men out to fight, a not-too-dissimilar number of hospital ships were now making the return journey with thousands of wounded soldiers at all hours of the day and night. With local hospitals in the Southampton area unable to cope with the numbers, once back in England men were being transported to their home towns around the country.

It was mid-morning by the time the convoy of military ambulances pulled into the grounds of Guy's Hospital, which was less than one mile from

Queen's Buildings. The relatives of the wounded waited with some trepidation to see their particular loved one, wondering what condition their son, husband or brother would be in. Among the dozens of families were the Williams of Queen's Buildings. All the impatient relatives had been herded into makeshift waiting rooms, from where they could see the incoming vehicles.

"If you just wait here," said an orderly, "we will check in all of the wounded men and then come back and call your name. We will then take you to see your relative."

The hour-long wait was excruciating; the room in which Charlie, Betty, Maureen and Mary sat was deathly silent. Each family looked up expectantly each time a hospital official intermittently entered the room: those called followed with a feeling of excitement mixed with fear, while those left in the room sagged their shoulders and resumed their wait.

Finally, the orderly who had shown them into the room in the first place appeared again. "The family of Private Leonard Williams?" he asked. The four got up and made to follow the man but before they moved any further, he said, "Private Williams has asked if he could speak with his sister first on her own."

They all stopped and looked at one another in surprise. "Why?" asked Maureen.

"I'm not sure, Miss," said the man, "he was just

quite insistent."

Maureen turned and looked at her parents and then at Mary; Charlie shrugged and nodded his assent. The three sat back down and Maureen left with the orderly, following along a series of corridors until they reached the appropriate ward.

"Private Williams is in the third bed on the left," the orderly said, and left to carry out his next task.

Maureen moved forwards as the wounded man turned to face her. "Hello, sis," he said.

Maureen's first reaction was to smile. "Reg!" she exclaimed, now believing that there had been some mistake and *both* of her brothers had actually survived. But the expression on her brother's face told her that something was horribly wrong and her smile dropped away.

"Where's Len?" she asked, quietly.

"Len's dead, Mo, I had to leave him in France." Reg started to sob and his lack of control saw him dissolve into a coughing fit.

Maureen rushed to her brother and held him. "Shhh, my beautiful boy." She was crying herself by this time. She now somehow knew what had happened but after a few minutes asked anyway.

"It was hell out there," recalled Reg. "We were sent to the front and ordered to go over the top. I had told Lennie about the Connors and before we went he said that if he didn't make it and I did, I should swap our identities. That way, if the police found out that I did them in – or should I say that Reg Williams did them in – we could tell them that Reg Williams died on the Somme. It was the only way to avoid the noose – Len reckoned if they found out the truth, I would hang for it."

"I wouldn't be surprised, knowing how this country works," said Maureen. "It's true that the police have already been round asking questions."

"Asking who? Asking what?"

"Some copper came round the house wanting to know where you and Len were the night before you went away. Big Scottish bloke from Scotland Yard; he was a lot smarter than the other coppers we normally see around here. I was told he's from North London."

Reg lowered his voice to a hush. "How did he know we were involved?"

"I think he worked out that it was everyone in the Queen's Buildings who had benefited from the Connors' deaths. I took some envelopes from work and pushed the money through their letter boxes. When he came round, everyone told the same story about receiving the money in a Woolwich Arsenal envelope. That was my big mistake."

"So it was me he was after then."

"What?"

"Oh, just something one of the sergeants said to me the other day. He had received a telegram from Scotland Yard asking for information about someone called Williams. He said he had a telegram but had lost it, so he wasn't sure who they wanted." Reg thought for a while and then referred back to the policeman. "This copper doesn't suspect you of anything does he, Mo? I would rather come clean with him than risk anything happening to you?" Reg coughed again in his excitement, as if he were an old man trying to clear his chest.

"I know he suspects me of helping by delivering the envelopes – he told me so – but he can't prove anything."

The two remained silent for a few minutes while Maureen tried to come to terms with the magnitude of what she was hearing.

"I don't know what Mum and Dad's reaction will be; we were all just coming to terms with losing you, now they'll have to go through the pain and agony again knowing it's Len that has gone." It was only then that something worse occurred to her. "And Mary! God, how will she cope with this? She believes her sweetheart is coming home."

It was at the mention of Mary's name, that Reg remembered his other instruction, issued by his dying brother. When he opened the drawer by his bed to retrieve the grubby envelope he had brought back from France, he also saw the ring John Mann had asked him to give to Maureen for safe keeping. Reg hesitated, wondering which item he should hand over first.

"What is it, Reg?" asked his sister, when she saw his hesitation.

"I've just remembered, I have something for you and something for Mary." He took the ring first and offered it to Maureen, "Do you remember John Mann – his dad had the bakers on Newburn Street?"

Maureen looked puzzled for a moment at the seemingly random question, "Well... yes...they moved back to Wales didn't they?"

Reg smiled to himself, "No they weren't Welsh, they were German."

"German? I thought you said they were Welsh?"

"No, it's...never mind, that's not important."

"Why do you mention *him* at a time like this?"

"Me and Len saw him in France?"

Maureen couldn't make head nor tail of Reg's garbled recollection. He tried to clarify it by reciting what John had told them at Le Havre.

"He gave me his ring and asked me to give it to you just for safe keeping"

"To me?" Maureen took the ring and looked at it, "Why did he want to give it to *me*?"

"Well, he was sweet on you wasn't he? You and him courted for a while he said he would come and collect it from you when all this is over."

"*Courted!* I wouldn't say courted. We went to the dance once or twice and maybe to the pictures but that was about it."

"Well, he seemed to think there was more to it

from his point of view and asked me to give you this."

Maureen looked at the ring that was inscribed, "JK? what does that mean?"

"That's his real name apparently, Johannes Kauffmann. Did he never tell you that when you were together?"

"No. And I wouldn't say we were together either. He was just a nice bloke from church who asked if he could take me to the dance."

"He's still a nice bloke. The problem is that he doesn't feel German or English – fighting for one, captured by another, nearly shot and now probably locked up in a prisoner of war camp. And sadly, his organ playing days are over as he lost part of his hand in an explosion."

"I can't accept this," said Maureen, "it doesn't feel right."

"Just take it, Mo, it's what he wanted. We can't do anything else with it."

Maureen was a little annoyed by the awkward situation she felt she'd been placed in. Her eye then fell on the grubby envelope her brother was holding.

Reg followed her gaze, "Len gave me this to pass to Mary."

Maureen reached out to take it but Reg held on to it, "There's something else I'm not sure you know about," he said.

"What's that?"

"Mary is expecting Len's child."

Maureen slumped back in her seat, aghast. "Bloody hell! How many more surprises are there?"

Reg felt guilty about bombarding his sister with so much astonishing information. He gave her time to think.

"You know something?" Maureen said at last, "I thought she had looked a bit peaky lately but then who of us hasn't? We've all been worried sick."

Reg held out the envelope to his sister, "Len asked me to make sure she gets this."

"What does it say?"

"I don't know, I haven't opened it. But I suspect he is trying to explain the situation to her."

"What situation?"

"Lennie not only wanted me to assume his identity in order to save my life, but he wanted me to look after Mary and their baby, you know just to make sure they stay safe and the baby has a dad.

"So, you will live with Mary as a family?"

"That's up to Mary but I think it's the only way. People in Kennington know who I am but they won't say anything to the police, especially after they benefited from the Connors' deaths. This way, I stay out of the clutches of the law and Mary and the baby have some support, although I don't know what state I will be in to work after this."

"What should I do now?" asked Maureen, trying to come to terms with the revelations of the last twenty minutes.

"Maybe you could prepare mum and dad by telling them that there has been a mistake and it's me and not Len who survived. Once they come in, I will tell them everything."

"And Mary?"

"I'm sorry, Mo, but I'm asking another massive favour. Could you tell her and give her the letter? I can't think of any other way to do it."

Maureen nodded silently, "I suppose it is better coming from me than anyone else."

CHAPTER

# 15

# MORE AGONY, MORE TRAGEDY

"What's wrong?" asked Mary when Maureen returned to the waiting room. "Can we go and see Len now?"

Mary, Charlie and Betty could see by the expression on Maureen's face that something was not right.

"He's not feeling very well after such a long journey. He's asked if we can all come back tomorrow when he'll be well rested. I've left him sleeping."

The three were clearly disappointed by this news but understood; they reluctantly agreed and went home to the Queen's Buildings in silence. Mary was ashen-faced as Maureen and her parents showed her to her door.

"We'll come round and see you later, Mary, love," said Maureen.

Charlie and Betty were both a little surprised by this comment as they didn't see any reason for them to call. They simply put it down to Maureen's naturally protective nature and followed their daughter to their own door.

Once inside, Maureen wasted no time in unburdening herself from the secrets she carried.

"Mum, Dad, there is something I need to tell you

that is going to come as a shock. It's not Len that's come back, it's Reg."

Betty collapsed and fell against a chair; Charlie moved quickly to stop her falling still further.

"I'll get a glass of water," said Maureen before she continued. She went into the back kitchen and returned with a glass. "There you go, Mum, I know this is a great shock."

"I don't understand," said Betty, taking a drink.

She and Charlie were both thinking the same thing: this was neither good news nor bad, it was just different from what they were expecting. They had still lost one son and were coming to terms with the injuries sustained – whatever they were – to the other.

"I'm sorry having to tell you like this," continued Maureen, "but I didn't know myself until I saw Reg just now in the hospital."

"Why did Reg ask to see you first?" asked Charlie.

Maureen hesitated. "Well, he has something else to tell you himself. Something that I *did* know about but didn't think I would ever need to share with you. It seems circumstances have now changed."

"What about Mary?" said Betty.

"I will go and tell her later. I know her mum and dad will be there but perhaps you could come too. I know she'll be devastated."

Charlie nodded, still dazed at what his daughter was telling him and wondering what other secrets his son needed to share with him.

After an hour or so – giving time for Charlie and Betty to come to terms with the news – Maureen suggested they go and speak with Mary. It was Arthur, Mary's dad, who answered the door and showed them through to the living room, where Mary – sobbing with worry – was being comforted by her mum. She knew something was wrong but had no idea what.

Doris and Mary both looked up when their three guests entered. The atmosphere was a mixture of expectation and trepidation. It was Betty who spoke to her childhood friend first. "Hello Doris, love, we thought we would come round – we've got something we need to say to Mary."

Maureen took over; she sat down beside her friend and took her hand. "Mary, sweetheart, I have something terrible to tell you."

"Where's Len?" asked Mary, openly crying by this stage.

Maureen looked at her friend and then took the grubby envelope, given to her earlier by Reg, from her pocket. "This is for you," she said, handing it over.

Despite its poor condition, the envelope remained unopened from the time Len had written to his love. Mary gently opened the envelope,

sobbing as she anticipated the contents. Inside, she found *two* letters.

Within seconds of reading the opening lines of the first letter, Mary looked up and screamed at the ceiling. Maureen knelt to comfort Mary, who couldn't control her grief; she was crying loudly and rocking back and forth.

After a while, she held up the envelope and managed to blurt out through the tears, "Did you know about this?"

Maureen scanned the letters, the second of which made a reference to Reg's crime. She decided not to reveal that she knew about this to the rest of the room. "No," she said in answer to Mary's question. She whispered in her friend's ear, so the others wouldn't hear, "I didn't know that Len proposed to swap places in order to save Reg. Reg'll hang if they find out. Mary, love, Mum and Dad have lost one son, please don't let them lose another."

So lost was she in her grief, Mary couldn't take in what Maureen was saying. "I've lost him! I've lost him, my wonderful Len!" she wailed.

Her short life with Len was flashing through her mind, which mercilessly tortured her with happy thoughts: their childhood, family get togethers, the first time he had told her he loved her, and the night they lay together for the first time three months ago. Everything was supposed to be so perfect – they would be together with their baby when Len came home – now this. Although they hadn't been married, Mary already felt like a widow at twenty years of age, her whole adult life ahead of her, alone.

Maureen looked at the letter again. "Reg told me about the baby," she said. "Len had told him."

This was another revelation to the two sets of parents. Betty and Doris started to cry, while Charlie and Arthur stared on in disbelief.

From one woman to another, Maureen's heart went out to her friend, despite her own sense of loss at the death of her brother. She had witnessed and actively encouraged Len and Mary's courtship, the big sister fussing and clucking over the younger couple. She was so proud of them, so happy that her brother had found such a beautiful girl. She couldn't imagine the thought of losing such a love. She tried her best to calm her friend down. "It's what Len wanted, it was his wish," was the best she could come up with.

The room was silent for a few minutes before Charlie attempted to invoke some pragmatism into the situation.

"We need to keep this between ourselves," he said. "We will go to the hospital tomorrow and speak with Reg."

"I don't want to go," said Mary.

"You don't have to, sweetheart," said Maureen, "not if you don't feel up to it."

The following morning, Maureen accompanied her parents back to Guy's and retraced her steps from the previous day to the ward where Reg lay. She suggested they go in on their own.

"I'm not sure if I can go in," Betty said, "I don't know what I'll find."

"Come on, love, let's see our son," encouraged Charlie.

"He's through there in the third bed on the right," said Maureen. "I'll wait here and give you a few minutes."

Charlie and Betty tentatively entered the ward, wondering what they were about to see. As they entered, Reg looked up from his bed and smiled. Betty burst into tears and rushed towards him, hugging her younger son.

"We thought you were Len," she managed to say through her distress.

The irony of his mother's words was not lost on the young lad. "I know."

Charlie moved forwards and wordlessly shook his boy's hand.

"Hello, Dad," said Reg at last to his father, as he fought to control his emotions.

"I don't understand any of this, son," said Charlie.

Reg waited a few minutes while they all composed themselves before speaking.

"I was caught in a gas attack and it's affected my lungs" – his narrative was interrupted by another few seconds of quiet coughing – "but there's something else that I need to tell you both, something that will explain the whole thing. I hoped it would never come to this but it seems there's no other way." He signalled for his dad to pull up two of the chairs that were stacked by the doorway before continuing. "My life probably depends on what I am about to tell you. I hope you won't think any less of me but I did what I did for everyone's benefit, and if I'm honest about it, I would do it again given my time over." He took a sip of water to prevent a further coughing episode. "It was me who killed the Connors the night before me and Len left for France."

"*What!?*" exclaimed Charlie.

"You must be mistaken, love!" said Betty.

She couldn't get the thought of her two little boys out of her mind: they had always been so close, so alike, people often mistook them for twins. They were both still children in their mother's eyes, her love for them was overwhelming. Len was not only the older of the two but the more sensible; Reg was the one who got himself into scrapes, never a bad lad but often headstrong and prone to making the wrong choices in the heat of the moment. Len was the one who usually pulled him out of whatever spot he'd got into. She still saw them as children; they *had been* children a few short years ago. But now this: her son was now telling her things that, even in adulthood, were incomprehensible.

"There's no mistake, Mum. How could I be mistaken about something like that? Maureen was at home when I came in that night. She helped me clean up. I took the money everyone had paid to the

Connors and Mo delivered it for me." He looked at his father. "What they did to you, Dad, was the last straw. I didn't want you, or anyone else, to be left to the mercy of those animals, so I took matters into my own hands. I thought I had nothing to lose, what with going to France an' all that."

"I can't believe it," said Charlie.

"I told Len what I had done when we were over there, and before we went over the top, he made me promise that if he didn't make it, I would swap our identities and it was then that Len told me about the baby. If *I* didn't make it, well, it wouldn't matter."

Betty started crying again at the flippant comment. "Sorry, Mum, I didn't mean it like that, but I think the police are looking for Reg Williams, not Len Williams."

Reg may have been haunted by his own memories but he wanted to try and ease the pain caused to his parents by referring to his brother.

"Mum, I was with Len when he died" – he started to cry, which set the coughing off again – "he wasn't alone," he said after composing himself. "He died a hero, knowing that we all loved him."

Betty sobbed into a handkerchief. It was left to Charlie to speak for them both: "You are both heroes, son. No one round here would criticise you for what you did and I am not going to either. I can't tell you how proud your mum and me are of you and your brother."

# CHAPTER 16

# A POLICEMAN'S LOT IS NOT A HAPPY ONE

It had been three weeks since Superintendent Lamb had made his flippant comment concerning the hanging of Reg Williams. Since then, social disorder had increased, with an increase in the attacks on resident Germans, while protesters and peace marchers occupied too much police time for Lamb's liking.

Rab McKenzie had followed his superior's orders in contacting the War Office. His initial telephone call was met with a stunned silence. Not because the murders the inspector was investigating were thought to be trivial, but rather the logistics involved in identifying a single soldier in a theatre of war, then extracting him from his unit and then shipping him home for questioning on the off-chance that he may be involved in the crime, was absurd.

"Do you know how many regiments are deployed, Inspector, let alone the number of men?" asked the man on the other end of the telephone line after he had comprehended what the policeman had asked.

Rab felt more than a little foolish in asking, and conceded the point. "Yes, I do. As a former military man myself, I can't imagine the scale on which you are operating at the moment. But I am obliged to ask, given the seriousness of the crime committed."

"Very well, Inspector," said the man with a sigh, "Private Reginald Williams, you say, of the Kennington Pals?"

"Yes, that's correct. If you could take some time to identify where he and his regiment are, it would be much appreciated."

"I'll see what I can do."

The phone went dead.

Rab's enthusiasm for the case was waning to the point that he secretly agreed with the War Office official that there was little point spending valuable time trying to find a single individual who – if he was still alive, and if he even *was* the man he was looking for – would be viewed by many not as a villain but as a hero for what he had done.

As the superintendent had been preoccupied with other matters since then, and Rab himself had been busy with a spate of looting in Holloway, he had let the matter rest until there was something firm to report.

Something *did* arise towards the end of the first week in September. Much to McKenzie's surprise, he received a telephone call from the man he had spoken to three weeks earlier.

"I think I have found your man, Inspector," said Sidney Lloyd triumphantly, seemingly pleased with his own investigation. "We have a Reginald Williams, part of the London Regiment. They are currently part of the Somme operation, based at their rest camp near Le Havre."

"Thank you, Mr Lloyd, that's very useful." Rab wasn't sure if he was happy or sad about the news, but felt obliged to pursue the matter. "Would it be possible to contact his commanding officer?"

"We could get a telegram to the HQ in Le Havre but I'm not sure when, or even if, it would reach the man's unit. What would you like me to ask?"

Rab thought for a while before settling on something that saw him doing his job but kept things suitably vague and non-committal. "Simply inform him that Scotland Yard would like to speak with him about a matter when he gets back."

"Very well, Inspector," said Mr Lloyd with a sense of anticlimax, "I'll get that away for you. I'll also send the recruitment papers over to you."

"That's very good of you, Mr Lloyd, and much appreciated."

After a week of not hearing anything back from the War Office, Rab read of the latest phase of the Somme Offensive. The Battle of Flers–Courcelette had seen the London Regiment contribute to the successful taking of High Wood. Like all successes, however, it had come at a major cost – hundreds of men lost.

Two days after reading about the battle in the newspaper, Sidney Lloyd again telephoned McKenzie. "Inspector, I have an update for you. In the recent fighting, there were five men named

Williams from the London Regiment involved: a captain, who avoided injury, a lieutenant and a corporal who were both, unfortunately, killed, and two privates, one who was also killed and one who is reported wounded and is due to return home. I don't have the date of repatriation yet, but as soon as I get it, I will pass it on."

"Thank you, Mr Lloyd, you've been very helpful."

As he put the telephone down, McKenzie knew there could never be a happy ending to this case, regardless of the outcome. He apprised Superintendent Lamb of the latest position and informed his superior that he would visit the hospital when the wounded soldiers returned.

It was the following Friday when a constable knocked and entered Inspector McKenzie's office. "Sorry sir, this note came for you when you were out" – he handed over a piece of paper – "it was from a chap at the War Office."

McKenzie took the paper that had the constable's scribble on it: "Williams wounded on the Somme. Will return to Guy's Hospital on Monday."

"The man said you would know what it meant," said the constable.

"Is this exactly what he said? Surely he gave you more details than this?"

From believing he had done his inspector a favour, the constable was now realising that he had failed in taking down all of the information. "Well, I was just writing it down as he was talking, sir."

"Did he give the Christian name of the Williams involved? Did he tell you the extent of the man's wounds?"

"He possibly did, sir, but I didn't think it was important. When he said you would know what it was about, I just scribbled down what I picked up."

"Get out!" shouted the annoyed McKenzie.

His annoyance was compounded when he tried to reach Sidney Lloyd at the War Office, only to find that he had been called away on a family matter. Rather than burden another official with finding out more information about the Williams who was to be brought home, he decided to wait and visit the hospital himself when the wounded soldier returned. Moreover, despite being a hardened police officer and military veteran himself, he found he didn't really have a great appetite for interviewing a man who may or may not have been involved in a domestic crime and who had just survived the horrors of the Western Front. He resolved to wait until the Tuesday to visit the hospital, thus allowing the man's family to be the first to see him on his arrival home.

On the day in question, McKenzie made his way to Guy's Hospital, in part wondering what or who exactly he was going to see. Rarely did he dislike his job but this was one occasion when he felt a churning in his stomach that gave him a certain amount of discomfort. Unknown to him, Maureen, Betty and Charlie Williams were already at the hospital, Betty and Charlie seeing their son for the first time.

Inspector McKenzie approached the front desk, identified himself and informed the senior-looking nurse that he believed a group of local wounded soldiers had arrived.

"Yes, they were brought in yesterday morning," she confirmed.

"Do you have a list of who the men are?" asked Rab.

"I don't," said the nurse, "but if you go down to the arrival station – down the corridor and second on the right – they will have the list of the latest arrivals."

The nurse was so matter-of-fact about the influx of soldiers, it was clear to Rab that such an intake was a regular occurrence, something that she and the other staff had hardened to over the past two years. He thanked her and followed her instructions.

The corridors and wards were busy with hospital staff, visitors, and wounded men being wheeled from one area to another. Rab took the second turning on the right and saw that a desk – over which hung a sign saying Arrival Station – was vacant. He looked along the corridor and saw that a nurse was attempting to comfort a group of people. It must have been the nurse who had left her station briefly and Rab decided to wait patiently until she returned. He then looked closely at the group and realised that it was the Williams family from Queen's Buildings: Charlie and his wife Betty and their daughter Maureen. Betty was crying loudly and the nurse was trying to calm her down; Charlie and his daughter had the hollow eyes of those deprived of sleep.

Because they were so wrapped up in their own anguish, and people continued to go up and down the corridor preoccupied with their own thoughts, no one noticed Inspector McKenzie watching the traumatic scene that was being played out before him.

"I'll get you a glass of water," said the nurse as she left them momentarily and started to walk towards him.

As she approached, Rab quietly identified himself and informed her that he was interested in one of the soldiers who had arrived the previous morning. "I'm sorry to pry, but I am investigating a matter of extreme importance. Would I be correct in assuming that is the family of a Private Williams?" he asked, pointing to the three who sat about twenty yards away.

"Yes," said the nurse.

"Is that Private Reg Williams on the ward?" asked Rab.

"No," the nurse replied, "I believe his Christian name is Leonard."

"Has anyone else been here to visit him?" asked

Rab, wondering why Mary Eames would not be here to see her fiancé.

"No, I don't think so. The family came with a young woman yesterday but it was just the patient's sister who went in to see him. She and her parents came back on their own today. Now, if you will excuse me."

The nurse left Rab to contemplate the confused scene, poured a glass of water from a jug on her desk and returned, giving it to Betty Williams before a colleague shouted for her assistance further down the corridor. One thing was clear to the policeman: one of the brothers was lying in a hospital bed yards away from where he was standing – but which one?

As the man's family were still coming to terms with his return, McKenzie hated himself for having to intrude on their torment, but knew he had his duties. He walked forwards. Charlie looked dazed and stared straight ahead, seemingly oblivious to everything around him. Betty sobbed into a handkerchief. Maureen, however, saw the inspector approaching – he sensed hatred in her eyes.

"What do *you* want?" she snarled. Her parents didn't react.

"Hello, Miss Williams; Mr and Mrs Williams," said Rab, touching the brim of his hat. "I believe one of your lads has been brought home?"

Again, it was Maureen who spoke. "Can't you leave us in peace?" It was clear that she wanted someone to blame for the loss of one brother and the debilitating injuries of another. "Have you got nothing better to do than to trample on people's grief? Do you enjoy this, Inspector?"

"I'm sorry that you and your family find yourselves in the position of so many, Miss Williams, but I am duty-bound to speak with your brother." The truth was, Rab *did* have better things to do and he would rather be doing any one of them right now. He persisted, however. "Can I ask why Miss Eames isn't here to see her fiancé?"

Maureen glowered at the policeman. "*Miss* Eames," she said, imitating the inspector's reference. "Mary is coming with her mum and dad later."

"So it *is* Len who is on the ward?" asked McKenzie, indicating towards the door.

For the first time, Maureen dropped her gaze from his, and nodded silently. McKenzie chose not to prolong the questioning; instead, he decided to go and speak with Private Williams himself. "Excuse me," he said, "and please believe me when I say that I am so sorry for your loss."

The ward had a dozen beds crammed in against the side walls, containing soldiers with various wounds and traumas: burns, broken limbs, missing limbs, some soldiers with bandages covering their eyes, others swathed in a Mummy-like gauze. The policeman had witnessed suffering in South Africa but, looking round the ward, he was struggling to imagine what fighting conditions were like on the Western Front. Family members crowded round many of the beds.

Rab turned to see one of the patients looking at him as if he knew him. He was little more than a boy. Glancing down at the board on the end of his bed, Rab saw it was the man *he* was looking for.

"Private Williams?" he asked.

"Yes."

Rab referred to the board again. "Private *Leonard* Williams?"

The patient paused, then answered, "Yes."

"I am Inspector Robert McKenzie of Scotland Yard" – the patient showed no surprise at the announcement – "and I am investigating some murders that took place in Kennington a few months ago. I was wondering if you could help me with a few points."

"I've been a bit busy in France," said the wounded man sarcastically, but before he could elaborate, Reg began coughing and reached for a bowl on a small cabinet beside his bed.

Instinctively, Rab reached across to help him as he spat blood into the bowl before leaning back against his pillow and sighing after the exertion. Rab hated himself for pursuing the matter but asked anyway. "I think the murders took place the night before you left for France, Private Williams. Can you remember where you and your brother were the night before you left?"

"This is outrageous, Inspector!" said the man in the next bed. "I am Captain James Palmer and this man saved my life and lost his brother in the process."

Just then, a senior military officer appeared on the ward and was immediately drawn towards the raised voices.

"What's going on here?" he asked.

Rab could see by the insignia on the soldier's epaulettes that he was a lieutenant colonel and instinctively showed the senior officer the respect commensurate with his rank. "I am Inspector Robert McKenzie of Scotland Yard, sir. I am investigating a series of murders that took place in Kennington in July and I believe Private Williams may be able to help with the matter. May I ask who you are?"

"I am Lieutenant Colonel Ronald Blair, depot commander of the London Regiment. I'm here to visit these heroes and thank them for their efforts. Who gave you permission to come here and question my men, Inspector?"

"Respectfully, sir, Scotland Yard does not need anyone's permission to investigate the crime of murder. I appreciate these are unusual circumstances but I am duty-bound to see the matter to its conclusion."

"I don't give a damn about Scotland Yard! If you want to speak with my men, you speak to me first. Who is your superior, Inspector?"

"Superintendent Clive Lamb, sir."

"Well, rather than upset everyone here, might I suggest I speak with him first and then you and I can resume our conversation. I will telephone him later and will see you in my office tomorrow morning at zero nine hundred sharp."

Rab knew enough about army protocol not to engage in an argument with a senior officer. Moreover, he knew that there was more than an element of truth in what Blair had said about the time and the place: people throughout the ward had all broken off from their own conversations to observe what was taking place around Private Williams's bed.

"Very good, sir," said the policeman to the soldier, and with a nod to all, he left, partly relieved that he could resume his investigation into the – by comparison – rather mundane looting spree in Holloway.

# CHAPTER 17

# CASE CLOSED

At nine o'clock the following morning, Inspector McKenzie was waiting patiently in the entrance of the Regimental Depot in Southwark.

"The colonel is waiting for you, sir," said the young subaltern who met him. "If you would like to follow me."

Rab followed the junior officer across the parade ground and into a building on the other side of the barracks. Climbing a flight of stairs to the first floor, the subaltern knocked on a door and entered.

"Inspector McKenzie to see you, sir."

"Thank you, Pritchard, that will be all," said Lieutenant Colonel Blair, rising from his desk. "Good morning, Inspector, take a seat."

"Good morning, sir," said Rab, acknowledging the offer and sitting down in front of the commanding officer's large walnut desk.

"Now, I spoke to your superior, Superintendent Lamb, yesterday upon my return from the hospital. While he gave me graphic details of these murders you mentioned, he also informed me that the deceased were suspected local villains engaged in illegal moneylending, black marketeering, robbery and, worst of all, praying on vulnerable women in your parish who have lost loved ones in the war. There is even a possibility that these Connors were involved in the murder of one of your colleagues. What is also apparent is that some of your colleagues in the police force may have known about these wrongdoings and yet they continued with their criminal activities unchallenged. Would that be a fair assessment of the situation?"

"That is a fair summary of the situation, sir," replied McKenzie. "I have had my suspicions for some time, although we have yet to uncover any real evidence that could have led to a conviction."

"So now you are seeking to interview a severely wounded man who has come back from the trenches and who, I believe, may not even be the man you are looking for?" said Blair.

McKenzie thought Blair would make an excellent defence barrister at the Old Bailey. "All of that is true, sir, but as I said yesterday, I am duty-bound to make enquiries regarding the matter. I should stress that I have not arrested Private Williams in relation to any crime."

"I should jolly well hope not!" cried Blair. "He actually saved the life of an officer who is now lying beside him in the next bed. Let me read to you a section of what the officer put in his report:

I was alongside Private Williams in the first line of the attack. We came under heavy machine-gun fire within the first fifty yards of the attack, losing over half the platoon, who were either killed or wounded. I then made shelter in a shell hole along with six other soldiers, ready to continue the attack once we had reloaded our weapons. I then gave the order to leave the shell hole and continue the attack. As soon as we left our position,we immediately came under heavy machine-gun fire again, whereby I lost five of my men immediately. I had received bullet wounds to both my legs and my left shoulder; only one soldier, Private Williams, escaped serious injury. After a few minutes, we heard the German counterattack and by that time the Germans were approaching our shell hole. A group of five German soldiers appeared at the top of the crater. One solider raised his rifle and fired into the mound of dead corpses just to make sure they were dead. I then witnessed Private Williams single-handedly killing all five German soldiers, three by bullet and two by hand to hand combat. Private Williams then also suffered the personal trauma of seeing his brother die from his wounds. We were then subject to a gas attack, Private Williams took it upon himself to carry me back to our frontline trenches under heavy machine-gun fire, while we shared one gas mask between us."

Blair repeated the words from the report looking directly into Mckenzie's eyes. "three killed by bullet and two by hand to hand combat."

Blair continued: "Do you know much about mustard gas, Inspector? It affects the lungs and, depending how long you have been in contact with the gas for, can kill you or, if not kill, can permanently damage most of your internal organs. Private Williams will never recover from his wounds and will be suffering in pain for the rest of his life, and why? Because he chose to save the life of another soldier."

Blair looked at Rab. "I believe you were a sergeant in the Border Regiment, Inspector? South Africa, wasn't it?"

"Yes, sir," replied Rab, surprised. "How did you know that?"

"Superintendent Lamb told me. I'm a veteran of that campaign myself. It was bad out there, wasn't it?" He didn't wait for an answer. "But from what I can gather, what these boys are facing in France is very much worse."

"I would probably agree with that, sir."

"Lamb told me he considers you his finest officer, McKenzie. And I can see by the way you conduct yourself, you were a fine soldier, too – one I'm sure I would have been proud to serve alongside."

"Thank you, sir, that's very kind of you to say so."

"Let me, therefore, speak to you as a soldier rather than as a policeman. Do you honestly think persisting with this line of enquiry against young

Williams is appropriate in the circumstances?"

Inspector McKenzie believed he knew what had happened in the Connor household that night and what had happened subsequently. He had looked into the eyes of many a guilty man in his time, and judging by the body language and the look on the face of the man he had seen lying in the hospital bed the previous day, he was sure that he was the perpetrator of the crime he was investigating. And if he *was*, then he was Reg Williams and it was his brother, Len, who had died. It was equally clear that his sister, Maureen, had aided and abetted in covering the crime up. Rab was certain, given time, he could gain a conviction and establish the Williams brothers had swapped identities, but who actually would gain from that? He could also see the matter through the eyes of Lieutenant Colonel Blair and, in the cold light of day, he didn't have the appetite to pursue the matter any further. As far as the world was concerned, it was Len Williams who had returned from the front and it was Reg Williams who had been killed in France. That was the end of it.

"I think you are correct, sir," he said to the soldier. "I don't believe the man in the ward is the person we are looking for. I will go to the hospital and let him know as much and I think we'll then leave it at that. Although, respectfully sir, I don't think awarding Williams a medal would necessarily be the best course of action." Blair glowered at the policeman's apparent impertinence. Rab continued, "I should explain sir that any publicity in the matter might not be in Private Williams's best interests. Newspaper reports, possible interviews and maybe even photographs. Given what has gone on between his family and the Connors, it might be better to keep his head down."

The colonel didn't respond but offered a hand, indicating that their meeting was over.

Rab left the office and Blair thought for a while before wandering over to the window. He looked down to see the inspector being escorted across the parade ground towards the gate. After he had disappeared from view, the colonel returned to his desk and took out a folder that contained a note he made the previous day at the hospital. When he had forbidden McKenzie to speak to his men, Blair himself questioned both Williams and Captain Palmer, as well as the doctor looking after them both. Private Williams was continually playing down his role and claimed that he and Captain Palmer simply helped each other back to the British trench. When Colonel Blair spoke to the doctor however, the medical man assured him that with the bullet wounds sustained by Palmer in the failed assault, it would have been impossible for him to make his own way back, let alone help anyone else. The doctor was in no doubt that Palmer's version of events was the more accurate and put Williams's confusion down to the inhalation of gas and the general trauma of being on the front line. He told Blair that he had seen many a soldier suffer similar bouts of confusion and amnesia following their return. Blair sat at his desk and wondered if this was truly the case with Williams. He smiled and put the file back in the desk drawer.

Rab made his way the short distance to Guy's once more. As he turned onto the ward where Private Williams was, he saw his man giving a small package to the nurse who had just left him a cup of tea on his bedside cabinet. He didn't hear what Williams said to the nurse but she nodded and made to leave. As the patient watched her go, his eye naturally fell on McKenzie, who was approaching. They looked at one another; they both knew what the other was thinking. Rab ignored his thoughts, however. "I've just spoken to your commanding officer," said Rab, without engaging in any pleasantries, "and after doing some further investigations, I wanted to inform you that I won't be asking you or your family anything further about the Connor murders."

"Thank you, Inspector," said the patient. "Do you know who did it, then?"

He was pushing his luck with the question, but Rab smiled anyway. "I don't think we'll ever know for sure, but it was likely to be one of the rival gangs that have sprung up since the start of the war. Can I ask if your sister and parents are here again today?"

"I think they said they would be coming along this afternoon."

"It's just that I would like to speak to them as well and thank them for their help with the matter, especially in these difficult circumstances."

"That's very good of you, Inspector. You'll find them at home if you want to go along."

"I think I'll do that," said Rab, turning to leave. He then stopped and looked back at the young man in the bed. "Your colonel told me what you did out there, saving the life of this man here." He pointed to Captain Palmer, who had been listening to the conversation between the two. "You're a brave lad, Private Williams. I have great respect for you, especially after you lost your brother. I just wanted you to know that."

"Thank you, sir," said the young lad, appreciating the comments of a senior official.

"Thank *you*, for all your efforts," said Rab, "and I'm sorry once again for the loss of your brother."

He left the ward and saw the young woman who had taken the small package from Private Williams a few moments earlier, sitting at the nurse's station. On the desk in front of her sat the package.

"Excuse me, Miss," said Rab, pointing, "can I ask what you are to do with that?"

The nurse looked up and then at the package. "One of the patients asked me to post it for him."

"Private Williams?"

"Yes, that's right."

"I've just been speaking to him. Perhaps I could take it and post it for you, I'm a policeman and I know Private Williams well."

"If you don't mind," said the young woman, somewhat relieved, "it would be one less job for me to do."

"No problem at all," said Rab, picking it up and seeing it was addressed to a Sergeant Lawrence at Catterick Garrison.

His final port of call that morning was to the tenements of Queen's Buildings. Knocking on the door of number 5, he contemplated the sadness this family were going through. He was in no mood to prolong it unnecessarily, nor was he in the mood for confrontation with the grieving people.

"Good morning, Miss Williams," he said, removing his hat as Maureen answered the door, "may I come in, please? I have some news that I think you and your parents will be eager to hear."

The initial look on Maureen's face when she answered the door and saw it was Inspector McKenzie was one of fear and trepidation; it suggested the policeman had worked out the deception or, worse, had gained a confession from her brother. Her expression eased, however, when the policeman's pleasant disposition suggested there was better news forthcoming. She held open the door and invited him in. Rab followed her through to the kitchen where Charlie and Betty sat with the same blank expression he had witnessed the previous day.

"Mr and Mrs Williams, I am sorry to trouble you again but I wanted to speak to you all personally. I've just come from the hospital where I spoke with . . . Len. I don't think there is a need to question him further. You can all consider the matter I previously spoke to you about at an end. Once again, let me express my deepest condolences for the loss of your son. Please pass my regards on to Miss Eames and I hope, as a family, you can learn to live with your loss. I won't bother you any further and I'll bid you good day." As he turned to leave, he noticed the picture on the mantlepiece of the two boys in their uniforms taken when they were at Catterick camp, and by the side of the picture was Charlie's grandfather's watch.

"That's a lovely picture of your boys, I'm sure you're proud of the both of them. Oh, and it looks like you found your watch, Mr Williams." Rab smiled.

"I'll show you out, Inspector," Maureen quickly replied.

Inspector Rab McKenzie returned to Scotland Yard and went directly to his office. He placed the package on the desk and, taking a sharp knife, slit it open to reveal a small box. Inside he found a small metal weapon, through which he could slip his fingers and curl them round, forming a fist.

Protruding from the small body of the device, which now fitted snuggly around the inspector's knuckles, was a three-inch blade. There was a small note in the box which read: "Thanks for the loan of this, Sarge, it came in very useful. Private Williams, Kennington Pals."

Rab smiled to himself before looking through his desk drawer and pulling out the two recruitment files concerning the Williams brothers, sent to him by Sydney Lloyd from the War Office. He compared the handwriting on the packaging and the note with the handwriting in the files. One was an exact match: Reg Williams.

He went to the morgue to find Doctor Spilsbury.

"Hello, Rab," said the pathologist upon the inspector's appearance. "What brings you down here?"

"Hello, Bernard." Rab took the push dagger from his pocket. "Regarding those Connor murders, could this be the weapon used to kill the victim with the neck injuries?"

Spilsbury took the dagger from Rab and studied it with amazement. "Good heavens, where did you get this?"

"Oh, it just turned up," replied the inspector evasively.

The pathologist slipped his fingers through the grip and simulated a punch through mid-air. "Yes, it certainly could," he concluded.

"I thought so," said Rab. "Thank you, Bernard, that's all I need."

Rab took the weapon back to the yard to be photographed.

He then repackaged the dagger and called at the post office, where he sent it on its way. He then returned to Scotland Yard and prepared himself, for the one and only time in his career, to lie to his superior officer.

# CHAPTER 18

# SOUTH LONDON - 1945

The second war to end all wars was over and London celebrated. A generation earlier, young men had left to go abroad and fight. But this second global conflict of the century had brought war to the capital itself, in the form of the incessant German bombing campaigns that had destroyed buildings and claimed over 20,000 civilian lives.

It was May, the sun was shining and people danced in the street at the Allies' victory. Retired police inspector Rab McKenzie had another thought on his mind, however, as he made his way to Guy's Hospital for the first time in almost thirty years. His old comrade from South Africa, George Davis, was in his last days, dying of cancer, and Rab knew this was probably the last time he would see his old friend.

Despite their almost identical career paths – from volunteer soldier to the Boer War then to the South African Constabulary and finally to Scotland Yard – the two were an unusual combination: George, the outgoing Londoner; Rab, the introverted Scot. George had been an accomplished accordion player in their old military days and loved nothing better than getting the lads together on a night out and having a sing-song; it would always take Rab a dram or two before he could be coaxed into joining them.

The trait the two *did* share, however, was a fierce loyalty and an uncompromising sense of honesty and integrity, and it was this that had brought them together. They had been friends ever since. It was George who put a word in for Rab all those years ago with the powers that be at Scotland Yard, and it led to McKenzie's successful career with the force.

Being ten years older than Rab, George retired long before the Scot but the two remained friends inside and outside the force. Upon Rab's retirement, a few years before this final meeting, the two went on a trip together to northern France to see some of the battlefields of the Great War and visit the cemeteries where hundreds and hundreds of Commonwealth War Graves were marked with those distinctive white tablet headstones. Their visit culminated in a trip to the Thiepval Memorial to the Missing of the Somme. While he was there, Rab couldn't help but scour the giant memorial for a name that had never left him since those events in Kennington in 1916. Among dozens of men named Williams, he found 4257 Private R Williams of the London Regiment.

"I wonder," he said out loud, shaking his head.

"What's that?" asked George.

"Nothing," Rab had replied, "just a ghost from the past."

Now, Rab was visiting his old friend for the last

time.

"We had some good times together, didn't we?" said George as he lay there in his hospital bed.

"Aye, we did that, George. I owe you a lot when I think back."

"No, you make your own luck in this life, Rab, and whatever success you've enjoyed, you've earned it."

Rab spent a couple of hours sitting with his old pal before George fell to sleep. He decided this would be a good time to leave him. "Safe journey, old friend," Rab whispered in his ear as he rose to leave.

He walked aimlessly through the streets on what was still a beautiful late afternoon. The feeling of joy and relief seemed to permeate from each house and on the faces of everyone he passed. Rab decided to walk back to Waterloo station and, by pure chance, he found himself in front of The George pub. Since VE Day, it seemed every pub in London had held one long party; and as soldiers returned home, so the party continued.

Despite the relatively early hour, the noise coming from inside The George suggested it was no different. Someone was beating out "It's a Long Way to Tipperary" on the piano, while voices could be heard cheering and singing along.

Rab smiled and thought of his old friend once more, knowing he would have loved such a scene.

Against his natural character, he found himself overcome with a desire to go in and raise a glass to one of the truest friends he had ever known. Inside wasn't quite as raucous as it seemed from the outside, but there was a decent number of patrons, given the time of day. A couple of soldiers were standing by the piano, singing along, a little worse for wear, Rab thought, but excusable in the circumstances.

He was on his way up to the bar to order a dram of whisky when, for no reason, he glanced to his right and then did a double take. Sitting with his back to the wall, looking directly at him, was a face Rab recognised. The man looked at Rab as if he knew him. For his part, Rab never forgot a face; the last time he had seen this *particular* face was nearly thirty years ago, in the hospital he had just left half an hour earlier. Then, it had been the face of a boy; now it was the face of a middle-aged man.

Rab put his journey to the bar on hold and went across to speak with the man. "Hello, Mr Williams."

"Hello, Inspector McKenzie, what brings you to South London?" The man spoke as though he had waited for the policeman's return since their last encounter.

"No longer Inspector McKenzie, just plain Mr McKenzie. I retired a few years ago. I've just come from the hospital where I was saying my own farewells to an old army pal of mine."

"*You* were in the army?"

"Yes, the Boer War before I came back and joined Scotland Yard. It was rough over there but I don't think it was as bad as what you lads experienced in France."

"Well, we've all got a story to tell, I suppose."

"Are you here on your own?" asked Rab.

"Yes, I can't work these days," the man replied, before dissolving into a coughing fit.

Rab waited until the man had composed himself before asking, "Speaking of stories to tell, there's one that I would like to share with you. Can I join you?" He received a nod and a half-smile in response, as if the man knew what was coming. "You wait there then, Reg, and I'll get us some drinks."

CHAPTER

# 19

# THE TRUTH REVEALED

Tony had his suspicions about what had happened between Mr Williams and his brother, and their relationship with his nan, Mary Eames, but he wasn't in a position to prove anything and he knew it would only be likely to cause further upset if he pursued the matter.

He attended Mr Williams's funeral with his mum and dad on a bitterly cold January morning, believing that the old man had taken his secrets with him to the grave. How sad it was, he thought, that so few people were in attendance: one or two neighbours that he vaguely recognised and the pall bearers from the funeral parlour and that was about it. The one person he did find it interesting to see was someone his mum identified as Mr Williams's sister, Maureen. She and his nan were inseparable throughout the morning, linking arms and constantly sobbing at their loss. He found himself wondering what the two old women would be thinking as they stood by the grave, watching the coffin being lowered into the bone-hard ground.

They all retired for the obligatory cup of tea at the nearby Greysteads Hotel – an establishment that made its living from funerals – and Tony's mum introduced him to Mr Williams's sister.

"Oh, he's grown," she said in reply, as women of a certain age invariably do, "the last time I saw you, you were in nappies."

The comment was met with the classic response of a smile and an embarrassed backward nod. "I'm sorry for your loss," he said, trying to change the subject. "Mr Williams was a good man."

The sombre gathering wore on and finally drew to a close when the few mourners that were present gradually dispersed. Tony's mum hugged Nan and said she would look in on her the following day.

Tony, meanwhile, returned to his schoolwork, preparing for his final exams and whatever adulthood beyond school had in store for him later that year. With this now taking his full attention, he gradually put his interest in the life of the Williams brothers behind him. Little did he know that he was destined to tie up all the loose ends he thought he had been left with following the old man's death.

Not long after Mr Williams's passing, Nanny Eames herself was taken ill and, as winter turned to spring, her condition gradually worsened. Tony's mum was spending more and more time visiting his nan before finally she was taken into hospital. It was as though – despite their unusual relationship – his nan struggled to cope on her own without Mr Williams. In the first week of May, Nanny Eames passed away. He found himself greatly upset by the passing of a woman who had played such a significant role in his life. He also felt for his mum, who had viewed her as her own mother throughout her life.

It seemed as though Mary Eames had been the one fixed point in their lives and her kindness and love had rubbed off, not only on them but on many other families in the Kennington area. As a consequence, come the day of her funeral, unlike that of Mr Williams, the crematorium was packed with people of all ages who came to pay their respects, his own good friend Mickey and his parents among the number.

As the curtains closed at the end of the ceremony to the strains of "Abide With Me", Tony noticed a man standing beside a couple at the back of the chapel. He was very old but tall and seemingly alert; Tony didn't think anything more about it as he lowered his head and paid his final respects. Mr Williams's sister, Maureen, and Tony's mum and dad then led the mourners out of the chapel to Greysteads. The old man Tony had fleetingly observed waited respectfully until the other mourners left, before joining the end of the line walking the hundred yards or so for the wake. Inside, the man took a cup of tea and sat down beside the couple he was standing with in the church.

"Who are those people, Mum?" asked Tony, "I noticed that old man on the left in the church."

His mum followed her son's gaze. "I don't know, love, he is not from around here, I can't say I recognise him or his friends."

Maureen was sitting at the same table and, hearing their exchange, looked across at the man. "Blow me down!" she said. "I think I know who that is."

She went over and stood in front of the old man.

He looked up. "Hello Miss Williams," he said, in his distinctive Scottish accent.

"Inspector McKenzie," she replied, "it *is* you!"

"Yes, it's been a long time and it's just plain old McKenzie now I am retired."

"I never expected to see you here. I'm sorry but I didn't recognise you at first! Did you ever get married or have a family?" asked Maureen.

"No, I never did marry," replied McKenzie with a smile, "I always thought it was a little unfair to subject a good woman to the life of a policeman's wife. I understand from Reg you never married either, Miss Williams?"

"No," replied Maureen, a little confused, "I didn't know you stayed in touch with my brother."

"Yes, the truth is that I stayed in touch with Reg after a chance meeting we had after the war. We often spoke on the telephone for years afterwards and occasionally even met up. I knew he died at Christmas but I had a nasty bout of flu over the whole of Christmas and New Year and the doctor told me not to go out. Sadly, I couldn't come to his funeral. When I heard of Mary's passing, I wanted to come along and pay my respects to them both."

It struck Maureen that the former policeman made no attempt to hide his knowledge of her brother's true identity. "That's very kind of you, Mr McKenzie," she said.

"I wonder if you wouldn't mind calling me Rab?" he asked with a smile.

Maureen returned the smile, remembering the various emotions she had felt towards the detective over fifty years ago. "Very well, Rab."

"And in return, perhaps I could call you Maureen?"

"I'd like that," she said.

"It's funny, life's twists and turns," said Rab. "It's times like this when you reflect on your own experiences and those of others. Perhaps, had we met under different circumstances, things could have been different."

"Perhaps," agreed Maureen, "I think that would have been nice. So much could have been different if I recall."

"Yes, I remember Reg told me that Mary's baby died in infancy?"

Maureen glazed over, recalling the tragedy. "Yes, they were horrible times that affected so many."

"Aye, that they were."

Maureen carried on, as if talking to herself rather than to Rab, "Len and Mary would have been so right for each other. As if losing Len wasn't bad enough, their baby dying was doubly cruel. I remember the day it happened as if it were yesterday. I had just received a visit from Father White at St Wilfred's."

She told Rab about how Reg had given her the ring belonging to John Mann. After much consideration, she had visited Father White and explained her discomfort. Given that John had played the organ at St Wilfred's, she wondered if the priest might get in contact with any churches in the Frankfurt area to see if the Kaufmann family could be located. She felt it more appropriate that it should be returned to the family home.

Several months after she had visited Father White – and the day on which Mary would lose her child – the priest visited to inform Maureen that he and the bishop had contacted their counterparts in Frankfurt who had tracked down the Kauffman family. They learned that sadly, John's wounds had turned septic in the POW camp and he died of blood poisoning before the end of the war. Apparently, in a scene similar to that witnessed in the Williams household, when they learned of Len's death, John's mother collapsed in agony when she was told about the death of her son. Maureen was saddened by the news but drew some solace from Father White when he told her that Frau Kauffman gained a little comfort from the receipt of her son's ring.

Rab spoke for them both, "That wretched war

– and the one that followed – will we never learn?"

There was an uncomfortable silence before Rab suddenly rebuked himself, "Oh, how rude, I almost forgot," he indicated towards the man and woman who were sitting beside him, "I beg everyone's pardon. Maureen, let me introduce you to Mr. and Mrs. Palmer."

"How do you do," said Maureen politely, her face betraying the fact that she did not know the couple, "I'm sorry I don't recognise you have we met before?"

Mr. Palmer smiled, "I don't blame you for not recognising me, Miss Williams but I recognise *you.*" The comment compounded Maureen's confusion: the man explained, "I saw you over fifty years ago in Guy's hospital. I was in the next bed to your brother when you came to visit him. It's where I first encountered Inspector McKenzie here also. He may be retired but his skills in detection are still as sharp as ever. He traced me and informed me that Len, as I knew him, and Mary had both passed away. I said I would like to join him in coming along to pay my respects to them both."

"That seems remarkably generous," said Maureen.

"Not really," replied Palmer, "I would never be able to thank your brother enough for what he did for me. He saved my life on the Somme all those years ago." He turned to the woman sitting beside him, "This is my wife Anna," the two women smiled at one another, as Palmer reached into his wallet and produced three small photographs, "and these are our two daughters and our grandchildren. I have enjoyed a long, happy life, Miss Williams. I would never have been blessed in this way had it not been for the bravery and courage of your brother. I will be eternally grateful to him."

Tony sat watching the moving scene from across the room, curious as to who the man was and what they were talking about. Maureen saw the young lad watching them and beckoned him over.

"This is Mary's grandson, Tony," she said by way of introduction. "This is Mr McKenzie, who knew us all a long time ago."

"Is that 'young Tony'?" asked Rab.

"Only my nan and Mr Williams called me that, how did you know?"

Rab chuckled. "Yes, Mr Williams told me about some research you were doing into his wartime career."

"Hang on a minute . . . Mr McKenzie? Were you a policeman around the same time?"

"I was."

"Now that's amazing! When I was doing some research at the library a few months ago, I came across a story about some murders and I'm sure your name was mentioned in connection with the investigation." His brow furrowed as he thought.

"Who were they again? Ah, that's right, the Connors, the Connor family. Is that right?"

Rab and Maureen looked at each other knowingly. It reminded Tony of how his nan and Mr Williams had used to look at one another whenever he asked what seemed to be an indiscreet question.

"Yes, that's right," confirmed Rab.

"Can I ask, did you ever find the killer?"

"The case was closed satisfactorily," was the ex-policeman's enigmatic reply.

The morning gathering ended just before lunchtime, and as people gradually drifted away, Rab and Maureen said their own farewells and promised to stay in touch.

A few days after the funeral, Tony's mum said, "I've got something for you, love. When I went to see your nan a couple of weeks before she died, she asked me to give them to you after she was gone."

She held out two items. The first was an envelope that was delicate to the touch; it was stained and so old that it was held together by only one side of the rectangle, giving the effect of it opening like a tiny book. Between the parchment pieces were two letters. "She said this was in connection with the project you were doing. Maybe you should take it up to your room and put it with the other papers she and Mr Williams gave you." The second item was a small box. "She also said that this was a gift from Mr Williams and that he wanted you to have it, maybe to pass on to your children and grandchildren."

Tony was dumbfounded for a moment, moved and humbled by the gesture towards him from these two old people in their final days. He did as his mum suggested and went up to his room to inspect the contents. He sat on his bed, carefully handling the letters that he proceeded to read silently.

*My Dearest Mary,*

*When you read this my darling you will know that I am no longer here on this earth with you. I want you to know that my happiest times were those we spent together and that I have thought of nothing else than being back in your arms and of us being a family with our newborn baby and growing old together watching our child grow. I am so very sorry that this dream can no longer come true. But remember you have been my one true love from the very beginning to the very end. It is now my only wish that you and our baby have a wonderful life and that all your dreams come true. Kiss our lovely baby to sleep every night for the both of us. Tell Mum, Dad & Maureen that I love them very much and I died doing my duty.*

*Till we meet again my darling Mary.*

*Yours forever Len xx*

*My Dearest Mary,*

*I must ask you for your biggest act of kindness, which could save the life of my brother Reg. I have no reason for you to sacrifice your future for the protection of my brother I can only ask for your understanding.*

*I am certain that you know by now the circumstances of the Connors murders and you have probably put the picture together that Reg killed them. I know the police have been asking questions already.*

*I am certain Reg will be found guilty of their murders and will certainly hang. I begged with Reg that if I were to fall and if it was possible, Reg will take my name and avoid the noose and now it's up to you my love to see our plan through. My mum and dad have already lost one son and Maureen a brother it would be cruel for them to lose Reggie as well. Reg has agreed that he will look after you and our child and I have his word this will be done. This is a very hard thing I ask of you my darling and I pray that this happens for all of you.*

*Yours forever Len xx*

Tony had never imagined that he would find out the truth but here it was, with all the loose ends tied up: why there was always something strange about the relationship between Nan and Mr Williams, why Nan had always talked about Mr Williams's brother with such affection, and why Mr Williams had become so upset when Tony told him about his research.

He tried to imagine for a moment what their lives must have been like – he couldn't, it was unimaginable. He simply smiled to himself at the dignity and stoicism with which these people carried on – role models and inspirational figures without ever knowing it.

Almost as an afterthought, he opened the small box and found a pocket watch inside. He took out the watch and held it by its chain in front of him. Seeing a small piece of paper inside the box, he unfolded it and recognised Mr Williams's handwriting.

For young Tony. This was my dad's watch, his pride and joy. Please look after it for me. 4257 Private R Williams, Kennington Pals, Queen's Regiment.

Tony wiped tears from his eyes, put the watch back in the small container and placed it, along with the letters in the box, with the other papers given to him by Nanny Eames a year earlier. He closed the box, slipped it back under his bed and vowed to keep their secret to himself.

HE whom this scroll commemorates was numbered among those who, at the call of King and Country, left all that was dear to them, endured hardness, faced danger, and finally passed out of the sight of men by the path of duty and self-sacrifice, giving up their own lives that others might live in freedom.

Let those who come after see to it that his name be not forgotten.

Private Reginald Williams

24th London Regiment

The Kings Memorial Scroll to The Fallen

BUCKINGHAM PALACE

I join with my grateful people
in sending you this memorial
of a brave life given for others
in the Great War.

George R.I.

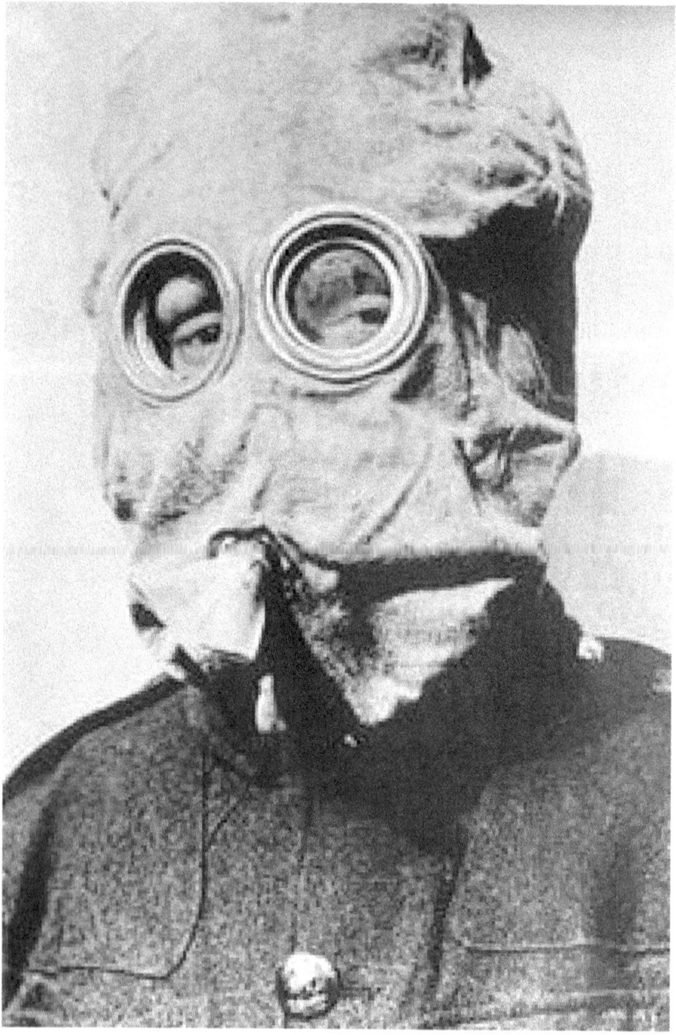

ww1 gas mask as used by Reg Williams
during the Somme Battle

Nanny Eames and Mr Williams at 5 Queens Buildings

# Epilogue

In 1974, Keith Daniel and a group of six archaeology friends from Canterbury formed the Men of Kent Detectorists Club. Numbers grew over the years until the club came to celebrate its twenty-fifth anniversary in 1999 with over twenty members travelling across the Channel to explore the fields of Northern France. Within an hour of the first morning of exploration, the control box on Keith Daniel's machine started to bleep. Keith dug down carefully with his trowel twelve inches or so and discovered what looked like a piece of metal wrapped around a wooden stick. After a little more careful digging and brushing, he found that it was a ring hanging from a skeletal finger.

The local gendarmerie was immediately called in before any further exploration could take place. After a cursory consultation with the local judiciary, it was quickly decided that the area was a First World War site and a proper dig should take place.

The detectorists were moved to another area and a week later, the French authorities commenced the excavation that revealed dozens of skeletons and weapons. Among the items found by the local archaeologists, the German Gewehr 98 and the British Lee Enfield were easily identifiable, as were cap badges, buckles and various insignia identifying soldiers from the 4th Royal Bavarian Division and the 24th London Regiment. But a single pistol found had the Frenchmen puzzled. They cleaned the weapon, took photographs, noted the serial number and sent the details to the Imperial War Museum in London and the Military History Museum in Berlin.

A few weeks later, the IWM contacted their French colleagues to inform them that the weapon was not a British army-issue pistol, but one that had originated from the London Metropolitan Police Force, the Webley Mark VI front-loading pistol.

The weapon was eventually returned to the Met's museum in Sidcup.

The museum's curator was Bill Dixon, who duly received and logged the newly acquired item. Upon checking its origin, Dixon discovered that the weapon was last issued to Inspector George Howard of Scotland Yard in May 1916 who was found murdered later that year. The gun went missing but a few months later, it was suspected of being used in the killing of a local villain called Billy Connor. It was this name that prompted the curator to make a phone call to someone he knew would be very interested in the discovery.

Bill was a career policeman who had risen to the rank of Detective Chief Inspector in his thirty years of service. Following his retirement he successfully applied for the role of curator of the Met Police Museum and had spent a further ten enjoyable years in Sidcup, where the Museum was based. As a young inspector, he had taken an even younger protégé under his wing: a young South London lad fresh out of school who wasn't sure what he wanted to do until he was inspired to join the force by some old boy who had served as a copper many years earlier.

From the moment he joined the force, the young lad used to plague Bill with the story of a case this old boy had been involved in, way back around the time of the First World War. Throughout his own career, he still talked to Bill about the case. Even now, with Dixon being the museum curator and the young lad having served twenty-five years in the force and himself climbing the ladder to the position of Detective Chief Inspector, he still badgered his old mentor about it.

Despite his one-time apprentice now being a senior officer, Bill always saw him as the young enthusiastic upstart he had groomed all those years ago. For his part, the DCI had the utmost respect and affection for his teacher and even allowed him and only him to use a playful nickname, once used by a man he had known as a child.

When he received the pistol from France, Bill called the DCI at Scotland Yard

"All right young Tony? How are you doing?" He asked, "You know that Williams-Connor case that you're always rabbiting on about? Well, you'll never believe what's just turned up?"

Tony just smiled to himself, "No let me guess," was his reply.

One week later, and ever the detective, Tony flew to France to find out just what else the archaeologists had uncovered.

A picture of young Tony the author

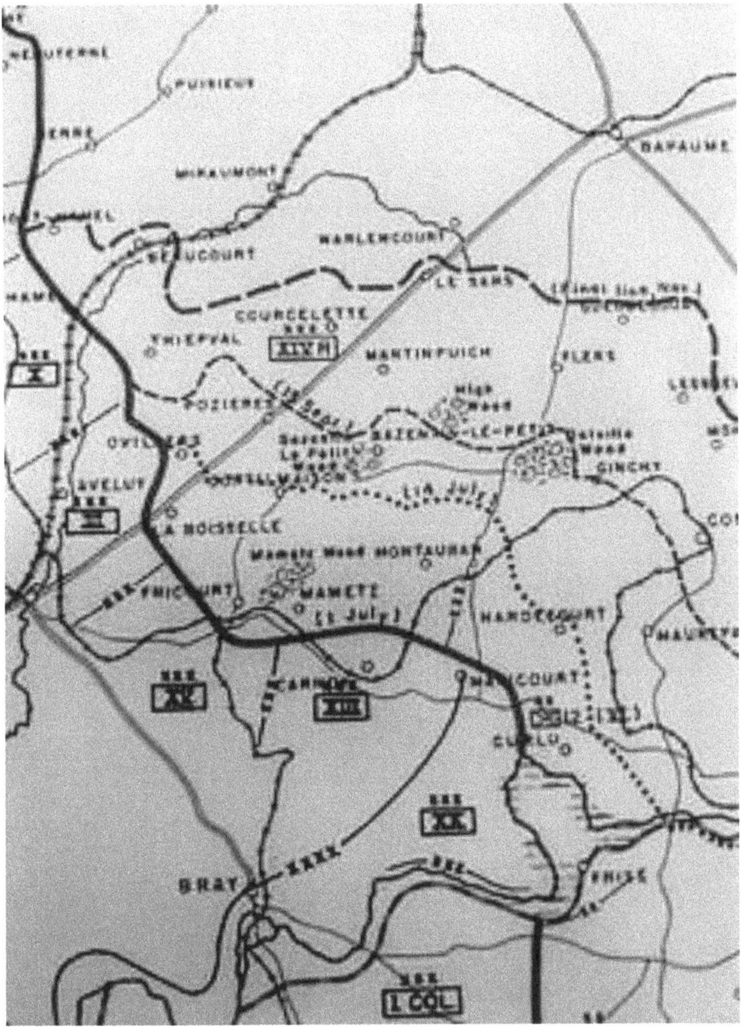


Highwood, where Len Williams was killed,
can be seen in the center of this picture

www.ingramcontent.com/pod-product-compliance
Ingram Content Group UK Ltd.
Pitfield, Milton Keynes, MK11 3LW, UK
UKHW050049141225
466001UK00005B/37

9 781835 636763